NOW EVERYONE
CAN READ AND UNDERSTAND
REVELATION
Without the Fear and Confusion

I0156251

NOW EVERYONE
CAN READ AND UNDERSTAND
REVELATION
Without the Fear and Confusion

*A*dvantage
BOOKS

JOSEPH T. L. LOH

Now Everyone Can Read & Understand Revelation by Joseph T. L. Loh
Copyright © 2020 by Joseph T. L. Loh
All Rights Reserved.
ISBN: 978-1-59755-606-4

Published by: ADVANTAGE BOOKS™
                  Longwood, Florida, USA
                  www.advbookstore.com

All Scripture, unless otherwise indicated, are taken from The Holy Bible, King James Version (KJV). Public Domain.

Scriptures quotations marked AMPC are taken from The Amplified Bible Classic Edition Copyright © 1954, 1958, 1962, 1965, 1987 by the Lockman Foundation. Used by permission.

Scripture quotations marked Interlinear Bible are taken from The Interlinear Bible, 1 volume edition Copyright © 1976, 1977, 1978, 1979, 1980, 1981, 1984 by Hendrickson Publishers. 2nd Edition Copyright © 1986 by Jay P. Green, Sr. Used by permission.

Library of Congress Catalog Number: 2020919115

Third Printing: February 2025
25 26 27 28 29 30 31   10 9 8 7 6 5 4 3

Table of Contents

INTRODUCTION

If you have ever watched a live telecast of your favorite sport, rooting for your favorite team or sportsperson, you most likely would have been on the edge of your seat, if you could even remain seated. That is because we do not know whether our favourite team or sportsperson is going to win the match, especially if it is the finals. However, if you already knew the outcome of the match, where your sports hero wins, you would be far more relaxed. That is why I love to watch repeat telecasts of matches. My favorite sport is tennis. So even if my favorite tennis player is two sets down in a best-of-five-sets match in a Grand Slam final, if I already know that he has already won the match, I could watch the entire match with a heart that is sure and settled. Why? Because he has already won! Even though it did not look like it when he lost the first two sets.

That is the reason God included the book of Revelation in the Bible – to let us know that we have already won! Isn't God marvellous? He took John the apostle up to heaven to show him all the things that must take place so that he could write it down for you and me to read and understand. We don't have to remain on the edge of our seats, wondering whether we are going to make it. God wants our hearts to be assured and settled when it comes to end-time events. However, that is not the case with many people. Rather than being assured and comforted, most folks get fearful and confused when it comes to reading the book of Revelation.

In my interaction with the body of Christ, I find that many are ignorant of what the Word of God has to say about end-time events due to various reasons. Some are plain frightened by what is written in the book of Revelation; some are put off by the language and terms used in it, and some are plain disinterested simply because they think that Revelation has no application in their daily lives. I don't blame them. Who cares about end-time events when we are struggling to pay our monthly bills or the rent for our homes? So ordinary folks think that this area of the Bible is best left to theologians, pastors and preachers. But it was God who included this book of Revelation in His Word. If God was the One who put this book into the Bible, then He meant for it to be read by everybody, not just Bible school students.

Another thing I notice when it comes to end-time events is that it tends to be sensationalized or hyped-up. This subject has been made into movies and books have been written on it for the purpose of sensationalism more than anything else. Now with the availability of various social media platforms, such platforms are inundated with video clips that come with all kinds of click-baiting titles regarding the Rapture and end-times. This does not help the believer to have a good grounding in end-time events. Rather, it leads to confusion and fear. "Am I qualified to be counted in the Rapture? Am I going to be left behind? When exactly does the rapture of the Church take place?" are some of the questions on the back of people's minds. So most folks shy away from this subject. But God wants us to read the book of Revelation as much as He wants us to read Psalm 23. He wants us to apply the truths found in Revelation to our everyday lives as much as He wants us to apply the truths of Psalm 91, Isaiah 53:4-5 or Mark 11:23-24!

Many books have been written on end-times, and while this book deals with this subject, it is not intended to be just another study on the subject of eschatology. This book is meant for *any person* to read and understand the book of Revelation. But that does not mean that we will skirt difficult issues surrounding the study of end-times. We will take the bull by its horns and resolve the seemingly hard-to-understand passages of Scripture. My primary purpose of writing this book is two-fold: *firstly*, to dissolve any fear or doubt that any person may have concerning the book of Revelation and end-time events; *secondly,* to apply the Scriptural truths learned here to our personal lives. Hence, I am not writing this book just to add to an already long list of books written on this subject.

Many think that if we study end-time events, we become too spiritual-minded and become of no earthly use. Some would say it is a form of escapism. On the contrary, when we have a clear and precise understanding of what God's Word says concerning end-time events, we become grounded and assured in our faith. We are no longer tossed to-and-fro by every wind of teaching on this subject. So having a good understanding of end-time events is not escapism. It doesn't make us spiritual weirdos. Instead, it will instil confidence in us and cause us to become mature, solid and unshakeable in our faith. We will live out our lives with purpose and focus. The Holy Spirit inspired John the apostle to write the book of Revelation not to frighten us, but to comfort and assure us, and put a smile on our face, just like the smiley on the cover of this book!

Chapter 1

IS JESUS COMING BACK?

The book of Revelation concerns events that will take place in the future. These events revolve around the return of Jesus Christ. Most Christians do not have any trouble believing that Jesus will return (although you will be surprised that some do). Nevertheless, let's do the needful and establish this basic truth: is Jesus coming back again? To answer this question, let us have a look at the following witnesses from the Bible.

THE WITNESS OF JESUS CHRIST HIMSELF

"Let not your heart be troubled: ye believe in God, believe also in me. In my Father's house are many mansions: if it were not so, I would have told you. I go to prepare a place for you. And if I go and prepare a place for you, I will come again, and receive you unto myself; that where I am, there ye may be also." (John 14:1-3)

"And, behold, I come quickly; and my reward is with me, to give every man according as his work shall be. I am Alpha and Omega, the beginning and the end, the first and the last." (Revelation 22:7, 12)

"He which testifieth these things saith, Surely I come quickly. Amen. Even so, come, Lord Jesus." (Revelation 22:20)

THE WITNESS OF THE ANGELS

"And when he had spoken these things, while they beheld, he was taken up; and a cloud received him out of their sight. And while they looked stedfastly toward heaven as he went up, behold, two men stood by them in white apparel; which also

said, Ye men of Galilee, why stand ye gazing up into heaven? this same Jesus, which is taken up from you into heaven, shall so come in like manner as ye have seen him go into heaven." (Acts 1:9-11)*

THE WITNESS OF PETER THE APOSTLE

"And saying, Where is the promise of his coming? for since the fathers fell asleep, all things continue as they were from the beginning of the creation. […] The Lord is not slack concerning his promise, as some men count slackness; but is longsuffering to us-ward, not willing that any should perish, but that all should come to repentance. But the day of the Lord will come as a thief in the night; in the which the heavens shall pass away with a great noise, and the elements shall melt with fervent heat, the earth also and the works that are therein shall be burned up." (2 Peter 3:4, 9-10)

THE WITNESS OF JOHN THE APOSTLE

"Beloved, now are we the sons of God, and it doth not yet appear what we shall be: but we know that, when he shall appear, we shall be like him; for we shall see him as he is." (1 John 3:2)

THE WITNESS OF PAUL THE APOSTLE

"For this we say unto you by the word of the Lord, that we which are alive and remain unto the coming of the Lord shall not prevent them which are asleep. For the Lord himself shall descend from heaven with a shout, with the voice of the archangel, and with the trump of God: and the dead in Christ shall rise first: Then we which are alive and remain shall be caught up together with them in the clouds, to meet the Lord in the air: and so shall we ever be with the Lord." (1 Thessalonians 4:15-17)

Based on the above Scriptures, the answer is a resounding "yes". The Lord Jesus Christ is definitely coming back. The statements of these witnesses will hold up in a court of law any time. They ought to lay to rest any doubt whatsoever that Jesus will return in power and glory. It is quite plain and evident.

However, the unanimous agreement of the truth of Jesus' second coming has been marred by disagreement on the timing of His return and the rapture of the Church. Some say that Jesus will come and take away His Church before the Great Tribulation, some say that it will be after the Great Tribulation, while others say that it will be in the middle of it. Better still, some say to prepare for all three eventualities! But that is being double-minded. The person who says that is hedging his bets. God's Word never operates this way. Scriptures tell us in James 1:8 that a double-minded man is unstable in all his ways. The Word of God is always decisive and precise.

So how do we prepare? The only way to prepare for the coming of the Lord is to have a precise understanding of Scriptures and to know with certainty what the Scriptures are saying about His return. So that is what we are going to be doing in this book. What we are *not* going to be doing is for me to state when I think the return of Jesus is and then try to back it up with Bible verses. Instead, we are going to look systematically at what the Word of God really says, allowing Scripture to interpret Scripture.

Chapter 2

THE DAY OF THE LORD

In this chapter, we are going to look at a passage in the Bible that provides us with the key that will unlock our understanding of end-time events.

*"For this we say unto you by the word of the Lord, that we which are alive and remain unto the coming of the Lord shall not prevent them which are asleep. For the Lord himself shall descend from heaven with a shout, with the voice of the archangel, and with the trump of God: and the dead in Christ shall rise first: Then we which are alive and remain shall be caught up together with them in the clouds, to meet the Lord in the air: and so shall we ever be with the Lord. Wherefore comfort one another with these words. But of the times and the seasons, brethren, ye have no need that I write unto you. For yourselves know perfectly that the **day of the Lord** so cometh as a thief in the night." (1 Thessalonians 4:15 – 5:2, all boldface mine hereinafter)*

The first thing that will take place is that at the sound of the trumpet of God, the Lord Jesus shall descend from heaven with a shout. The second thing to happen will be that the dead in Christ shall rise. The third thing that follows is that believers that are still alive on the earth shall be caught up (otherwise known as the Rapture) and join the dead in Christ that have risen to meet Jesus in the air. The apostle Paul goes on to state in 1 Thessalonians 5:2 that all these things – Christ's descent from heaven, the resurrection of the dead in Christ, and the rapture of the Church – shall take place on the Day of the Lord.

Did you get that? These three events all take place on the Day of the Lord. It is absolutely crucial that we get this truth as this is *the key* that unlocks everything else in the study of end-times. With this knowledge, we can now say with absolute certainty that the rapture of the Church occurs on the Day of the Lord. This is the first key fact.

I cannot over-emphasize how critical this first key fact is. This is the most important thing you should know about the second coming of Jesus. It is the key phrase that will help us understand the sequence of events relating to the second coming of Christ. The apostle Paul was not the only person that used this phrase. Peter used it too in 2 Peter 3:10:

> *"But **the day of the Lord** will come as a thief in the night; in the which the heavens shall pass away with a great noise, and the elements shall melt with fervent heat, the earth also and the works that are therein shall be burned up." (2 Peter 3:10)*

This leads us to the second key fact – the second coming of Jesus Christ is called the Day of the Lord.

The reason for so much confusion in the Body of Christ is attributed to the fact that we have not understood these two crucial key facts in the study of end-times. We need to get this clear because there are many verses in the Old Testament concerning this Day and these passages of Scripture will open up and show us some basic truths which will help us get all our confusions cleared up.

Having understood that the second coming of Jesus is called the Day of the Lord, let us look at a very important verse in the Old Testament that will give us the time sequence:

> *"The sun shall be turned into darkness, and the moon into blood, **before** the coming of the great and awesome **day of the LORD**." (Joel 2:31)*

The word *'before'* in this verse is a time sequence word. It tells us that prior to the Day of the Lord, something will take place in the heavens.

Joel 3:14-15 reiterates this fact:

> *"For **the day of the LORD** is near in the valley of decision, the sun and moon will grow dark, and the stars will diminish their brightness." (Joel 3:14-15)*

This sign in the heavens will draw the attention of all men toward the heavens. There will not be a single light in the sky that day as the sun, the moon, and the stars will stop shining. We shall call this the Blackout in the heavens.

Finally, let us take a look at a passage in Acts chapter one to establish a very important and foundational truth.

"And while they looked stedfastly toward heaven as he went up, behold, two men stood by them in white apparel; which also said, Ye men of Galilee, why stand ye gazing up into heaven? **this same Jesus**, *which is taken up from you into heaven,* **shall so come in like manner** *as ye have seen him go into heaven." (Acts 1:10-11)*

This Scripture assures us that the return of Jesus is going to be a physical appearance. We are going to see Him coming back the same way the disciples saw Him going up. We will examine this more thoroughly in due course.

Chapter 3

PRELUDE TO THE SEVEN SEALS

Things are going to get interesting in this chapter. We are going to look at the seven seals mentioned in the book of Revelation. We need to study these seven seals very carefully because one of the greatest confusions in the Body of Christ today is caused by the interpretation, or rather, the misinterpretation of these seals.

THE KEY TO UNDERSTANDING THE SEVEN SEALS

We must first look at the background behind the opening of these seven seals. By doing so, you will find the key and with this key, you can unlock the mystery and begin to interpret the seals. Once we have the key, it becomes easy. Otherwise, it is like banging on the door very hard without it budging. However, the moment you have a key that will unlock the door, you can then enter through it and you will begin to see things as they really are.

THE APOSTLE JOHN BEING TAKEN UP TO HEAVEN

To look at the background to the seven seals, we must begin with the fourth chapter of Revelation:

"After these things I looked, and behold, a door standing open in heaven. And the first voice which I heard was like a trumpet speaking with me, saying, 'Come up here, and I will show you things which must take place after this.' Immediately I was in the Spirit; and behold, a throne set in heaven, and One sat on the throne." (Revelation 4:1-2)

The reason John was called up to heaven was because God was going to give him a preview of the future. Many people read this verse of Scripture and interpret it to be the rapture of the Church because of the word "trumpet" being mentioned. They compare John being caught up to heaven as a type of the Church being raptured. So there are many people who say that the Church is raptured in Revelation 4:1 and then chapters five to eighteen are all talking about the period of the Great Tribulation.

First of all, we must realize that not every trumpet is the last trumpet! It is only at the last trumpet that the dead in Christ shall rise:

*"In a moment, in the twinkling of an eye, at the **last trump**: for the trumpet shall sound, and the dead shall be raised incorruptible, and we shall be changed." (1 Corinthians 15:52).*

Here it simply tells us that when John heard God speak to him, it sounded *like* a trumpet. God was asking John to come up because He wanted to show him future events. In verse two, John went up in the Spirit. That alone should indicate to us that this cannot be a type of the Rapture as the Rapture is the catching away of the physical body. We will deal more with this topic later on.

THE BOOK THAT WAS SEALED

With the aforementioned background in mind, we can now proceed to read the fifth chapter of Revelation:

"And I saw in the right hand of him that sat on the throne a book written within and on the backside, sealed with seven seals. And I saw a strong angel proclaiming with a loud voice, Who is worthy to open the book, and to loose the seals thereof? And no man in heaven, nor in earth, neither under the earth, was able to open the book, neither to look thereon. And I wept much, because no man was found worthy to open and to read the book, neither to look thereon." (Revelation 5:1-4)

Now, let's take a moment and ask ourselves one question – what does this book that is sealed with seven seals represent? To get the answer, we need to look at Isaiah 29:10-11.

"For the LORD hath poured out upon you the spirit of deep sleep, and hath closed your eyes: the prophets and your rulers, the seers hath he covered. And the vision of all is become unto you as the words of a book that is sealed, which men deliver to one that is learned, saying, Read this, I pray thee: and he saith, I cannot; for it is sealed." (Isaiah 29:10-11)

God said in Isaiah chapter twenty-nine that the people of Israel have no vision and no understanding. Isaiah said that the vision of the seers and the prophets was like a book that was sealed so that no man could read and no one could look into it. Therefore this book that was sealed with the seven seals must also represent the events of the future that God has already decided would take place. The fact that it was sealed implies that it has not yet been revealed to man.

What is the one thing we do not know? We do not know the future. Here is a book of prophecy revealing the things that will soon happen. That really was the purpose of John being taken up to Heaven. God wanted to show him the future from the book, and one could imagine that John was getting pretty excited about being shown the events that would take place in the future. Wouldn't you? But when he realised that nobody was found worthy to open the book that was all sealed up, he began to lament and weep.

Then one of the twenty-four elders comforted him and told him not to despair.

"But one of the elders said to me, 'Do not weep. Behold, the Lion of the tribe of Judah, the Root of David, has prevailed to open the scroll and to loose its seven seals.'" (Revelation 5:5)

Who is this Lion of the tribe of Judah? We need to understand this verse very carefully because this verse is the key to our understanding of the seven seals. The thirty-first chapter of Isaiah tells us that when the Lord comes and fights for Israel, He will be fierce like a lion and He will not be afraid of all the shepherds that will shout against Him.

"For thus hath the Lord spoken unto me, Like as the lion and the young lion roaring on his prey, when a multitude of shepherds is called forth against him, he will not be afraid of their voice, nor abase himself for the noise of them: so

shall the Lord of hosts come down to fight for mount Zion, and for the hill thereof." (Isaiah 31:4)

Revelation 5:5 also states that this Lion of the tribe of Judah is the Root of David. In other words, before David existed, this person already was. It's quite obvious that this is none other than Jesus Himself.

You see, the prophetic future was sealed and only God Almighty knows the future. But Jesus, the Son of the living God, has prevailed to open the seven seals of the book that will reveal what future events will unfold. In other words, Jesus Christ is the one revealing the future.

With the above in mind, let us turn to twenty-fourth chapter of the gospel of Matthew. Have a look at verse three:

"And as He sat upon the mount of Olives, the disciples came unto Him privately, saying, Tell us, when shall these things be? And what shall be the sign of Thy coming, and of the end of the world?" (Matthew 24:3)

Just as curious as anyone else, the twelve disciples wanted to know what will take place in the future. Being ordinary people like you and me, they did not know the future as it was hidden from them. So they did the most logical thing – they came to Jesus privately and asked Him to show them. What did Jesus do? He simply obliged and proceeded to tell them in plain, easy-to-understand language. Jesus did not berate them nor withhold any information from them. Isn't our Lord wonderful? He is so approachable and amenable.

Remember what we established earlier on from Revelation 5:5? It is none other than Jesus Christ who is going to reveal the future by opening the seven seals of the book. And here in Matthew chapter twenty-four, we have Jesus revealing the future to the disciples in plain words. Do you notice anything striking here? It is **the one and same person** unfolding the secret of the future both in Revelation chapter six and Matthew chapter twenty-four. This is your key to understanding the seven seals, because Jesus will never contradict Himself. With this crucial information in mind, we shall proceed to examine each of the seven seals in the next chapter.

Chapter 4

OPENING OF THE FIRST FOUR SEALS

THE FIRST SEAL

"And I saw when the Lamb opened one of the seals, and I heard, as it were the noise of thunder, one of the four beasts saying, Come and see. And I saw, and behold a white horse: and he that sat on him had a bow; and a crown was given unto him: and he went forth conquering, and to conquer." (Revelation 6:1-2)

The first seal depicts a rider seated on a white horse, having a bow and a crown. There are so many interpretations for this very first seal. Some say that the rider is Christ because He comes riding on a white horse. After all, Revelation 19:11 shows us Jesus coming on a white horse. So some folks conclude that this rider must be Jesus. There are also those who postulate that this rider is the Antichrist. Why? Because he carries a bow whereas Christ comes with a sword and the sword is the Word of God that proceeds out of His mouth. Since Christ never carries a bow, they say that this is the Antichrist. Then again, there are also those that propound that this is the gospel. They say that the gospel of Jesus Christ is like the rider going forth to all the nations of the world conquering and to conquer. So if you pick twenty different books written on the book of Revelation, you will get about ten different interpretations on this one little rider on a white horse!

Now, we have established in the previous chapter that the key to understanding the seven seals lies in the fact that it is Jesus revealing future events. He is showing us the future by opening up the seals. Back in the twenty-fourth chapter of the gospel of Matthew, Jesus is also the one revealing the future to the disciples. As I said in the previous chapter, Jesus will never contradict Himself. It behoves us then to go back and see what Jesus said in Matthew chapter twenty-four and compare it with the First Seal.

But before we do that, let us use our God-given common sense and examine this rider on the white horse. This rider has a bow, but it does not say that he has any arrow. Well, if you carry a bow and you have no arrows, it is like carrying a gun without any bullets. Let's say a burglar breaks into a person's home and he brandishes a gun at the homeowner. He threatens the homeowner that he will shoot him or her if he or she did not hand over to him all his or her valuables. However, there are no bullets inside the gun. What is the burglar trying to do? Deceive the owner!

Now, let's see what Jesus says in Matthew 24:4-5:

*"And Jesus answered and said unto them, Take heed that no man **deceive** you. For many shall come in my name, saying, I am Christ; and shall deceive many." (Matthew 24:4-5)*

The first thing that Jesus mentioned is deception! Jesus was telling His disciples that deception will have its way in the world and many people will be deceived by those that go forth in His name. The first event of the future, the rider on the white horse, in Revelation 6:1-2 and the first thing that Jesus mentioned in Matthew chapter twenty-four is **deception**.

Jesus is in fact warning us about those that purport to come in His name. They are like the rider upon the white horse. White is the symbol for purity. Christ comes riding on a white horse because righteousness is His girdle. So here we have those who come in the name of Christ, all dressed up in Christian garments and using Christian language but they are not of Christ.

Since the late nineteenth century and the beginning of the twentieth century, we have seen the beginning of all the false cults. We saw the mushrooming of the Jehovah Witnesses, the Christian Scientists, Mormons, Unification Church, et cetera, all within the previous century. All these cults have millions of followers today. Reverend Sun Myung Moon, who founded the Unification Church in Korea, claimed that Jesus Christ has already come and that we do not need to wait for Him to come. He quoted Matthew 24:27 and said that since the Bible says that "as the lightning shineth from the east to the west, so also will the coming of the Son of man be," Christ shall therefore come from the east and that must surely mean Korea. Hence he claimed that he is the Christ that has already come! There are millions of people today in the world that are his followers. Jesus has said that many will come in His name claiming to be Christ and shall deceive many. This is the rider on the white horse and he has already gone forth conquering and to conquer.

Notice the similarity of the words used here:

Revelation 6:2	–	"conquering and to conquer"
Matthew 24:5	–	"and shall deceive many"

"For many will come in My name saying I am Christ." All white and very Christian-looking and very much like Jesus but not everyone who claims to come in the name of the Lord is from God and of God. Take the organization called the "Church of Jesus Christ of the Latter-Day Saints" for instance. Sounds like a great name for a church. But they are the Mormons. Their founder, Joseph Smith, secretly taught and practised polygamy amongst many other deviant doctrines. His leaders also taught that God the Father had a plurality of wives and Christ had multiple wives. Now that is deception. Yet the followers of Joseph Smith can be counted by the millions. The followers of Jehovah Witnesses are also in the millions. Today in the 21st century, many more false Christs have mushroomed all over the world. Why? The simple answer is deception. They all sound and look like Christians but are really leading men and women away from the truth. Deception brings people into bondage. Bondage brings people into sorrows and hurts.

We would be remiss if we think that deception is just limited to cults. Deception occurs when you get swept away by a wrong idea (no matter how valid it may appear to be), but you have become convinced that it is truth. There is a fine line between something that is valid and something that is true. Something that is valid is not necessarily absolute. That is the reason why Jesus warned us to *"take heed that **no man** deceive you"*.

THE SECOND SEAL

"And when he had opened the second seal, I heard the second beast say, Come and see. And there went out another horse that was red: and power was given to

him that sat thereon to take peace from the earth, and that they should kill one another: and there was given unto him a great sword." (Revelation 6:3-4)

The Second Seal has a horse that is red. Again, let's employ our Holy Spirit-breathed common sense. What is red in colour? It is the colour of blood. Power is given to the rider to take away peace from the earth. What happens when you take away peace? You have war! Much blood is spilled in a war. The verse goes on to say *"that they should kill one another: and there was given unto him a great sword."* It is quite obvious we are talking about war here. It's almost self-explanatory.

Nevertheless, let's go back to Matthew chapter twenty-four and see what Jesus said next:

*"And ye shall hear of **wars and rumours of wars**: see that ye be not troubled: for all these things must come to pass, but the end is not yet. For nation shall rise against nation, and kingdom against kingdom…" (Matthew 24:6-7)*

Look at that! The second thing that Jesus mentioned, after He spoke about deception, is war. Just take a look at the words used in Revelation and Matthew:

Revelation 6:3-4 – "they should kill one another"

Matthew 24:6-7 – "nation shall rise against nation, kingdom against kingdom"

Jesus used plain words in Matthew chapter twenty-four to tell us that people shall kill one another. One does not have to be a historian to know the sheer number of wars fought in just the twentieth and twenty-first centuries compared to past centuries. The First World War started at the beginning of the twentieth century. The Second World War ended in the year 1945. After that, the United Nations was formed to prevent wars. But more wars have been fought ever since. All we need to do is to have a look at the number of wars and battles fought on multiple fronts in the Middle East, let alone the rest of the world.

Today, thanks to the Internet and online news, not only do we hear of wars but also rumours of wars. What are we seeing? The Second Seal has been opened. The rider on the red horse has gone out. He has taken away peace and we are seeing wars and battles all over the world.

THE THIRD SEAL

"And when he had opened the third seal, I heard the third beast say, Come and see. And I beheld, and lo a black horse; and he that sat on him had a pair of balances in his hand. And I heard a voice in the midst of the four beasts say, A measure of wheat for a penny, and three measures of barley for a penny; and see thou hurt not the oil and the wine." (Revelation 6:5-6)

The third horse here is a black horse. White is the symbol of purity and red is the colour of blood. What does black symbolize? Black symbolizes sorrow and mourning. That is why people wear black during funerals.

The rider had a pair of balances in his hand. Balances were what people used to measure the weight of foodstuff. The verse goes on to say, "A measure of wheat for a penny, and three measures of barley for a penny." The Greek word for *penny* is the word *denarius*. In the time of apostle John, one denarius was a day's wage for a labourer. A denarius could buy you sixteen measures of wheat and sixty-four measures of barley. But here it says a measure of wheat for a denarius, and three measures of barley for a denarius. Why? Only one condition can bring about such a scenario – scarcity brought about by famine.

Now let's turn to the second part of Matthew 24:7 to see what Jesus said:

"…and there shall be famines…" (Matthew 24:7)

Isn't that amazing? Right after Jesus talked about deception and war, the third thing He mentioned is famine!

I think I don't have to educate the reader as to the countless number of famines that have occurred in the twentieth and twenty-first centuries. Some famines are due to natural causes and some are man-made. Famine is very real in many countries because of drought. Famine is very real in many countries because of political mismanagement (just take a look at Venezuela and North Korea). Famine is very real in many countries because of war.

The Third Seal has been opened and the rider upon the black horse has gone forth.

THE FOURTH SEAL

"And when he had opened the fourth seal, I heard the voice of the fourth beast say, Come and see. And I looked, and behold a pale horse: and his name that sat on him was Death, and Hell followed with him. And power was given unto them over the fourth part of the earth, to kill with sword, and with hunger, and with death, and with the beasts of the earth." (Revelation 6:7-8)

This fourth horse is pale in colour. Well, when you look at a human corpse, it looks pale, right? The rider's name is Death. The rest of this verse is self-explanatory and does not really need any interpretation. It is obviously talking about death. You know, one of the reasons we believers get into such doctrinal mess is because we over-interpret and read too much into a verse. But I digress.

What's the fourth thing that Jesus mentioned in Matthew 24:7?

"….and pestilences, and earthquakes, in divers places." (Matthew 24:7)

Jesus spoke about pestilences and earthquakes in various places in the world. Pestilences and earthquakes result in death.

What are pestilences? The Merriam-Webster dictionary defines pestilence as: "a contagious or infectious epidemic disease that is virulent and devastating; something that is destructive or pernicious". In other words, plagues. Again, it is moot for me to spell out the countless number of plagues that have emerged in this century and the last one. One can just do a search for it online and you will see a long list of epidemic diseases that have plagued this earth. We had the bubonic plague, AIDS (acquired immune deficiency syndrome), SARS (Severe Acute Respiratory Syndrome), MERS (Middle East Respiratory Syndrome), H1N1 influenza (swine flu), the bird flu, the ebola epidemic, just to name a few. Need I mention the Covid-19 (SARS-CoV-2) pandemic that has paralyzed almost the entire world? Most countries remain in total or partial lockdown as this book is being written. Millions have died from such diseases.

As for earthquakes, it is virtually impossible to list out all the earthquakes and tsunamis in the twentieth and twenty-first centuries alone. Again, one just has to search for it online and you will be inundated with recent occurrences of earthquakes and tsunamis that have claimed thousands upon thousands of lives, conservatively speaking. We can safely conclude that the Fourth Seal has been opened.

THE BEGINNING OF SORROWS

I want you to notice something very interesting here. Jesus said in Matthew 24:8: *"All these are the beginning of sorrows."* In other words, Jesus grouped all the four events enumerated above into one group. He said that all these four events are the beginning of sorrows.

Now, in Revelation chapter six, you will notice that the First Seal to the Fourth Seal are all riders on horses! Do you see the parallelism here? Fascinating, isn't it? As I mentioned earlier, Jesus never contradicts Himself. It is Jesus revealing the future in Matthew chapter twenty-four and it is Jesus revealing the future in Revelation chapter six. This alone ought to prove the accuracy and veracity of the Word of God beyond any shadow of doubt.

As mentioned earlier, the book of Revelation uses symbolic language. So Jesus grouped the events of the first four seals into one category of riders on horses. In Matthew chapter twenty-four, Jesus used plain language, and He grouped these four events into one category and called it the Beginning of Sorrows. However, Jesus also said that the end is not yet (Matthew 24:6). Jesus said it is only the beginning. If there is a beginning of sorrows, there will also be a climactic ending of sorrows.

We still have three more seals to open. In the next chapter, we are going to look at the Fifth Seal which is the most crucial period that the entire Body of Christ will face.

Chapter 5

OPENING OF THE FIFTH SEAL

THE FIFTH SEAL

"And when he had opened the fifth seal, I saw under the altar the souls of them that were slain for the word of God, and for the testimony which they held: And they cried with a loud voice, saying, How long, O Lord, holy and true, dost thou not judge and avenge our blood on them that dwell on the earth? And white robes were given unto every one of them; and it was said unto them, that they should rest yet for a little season, until their fellowservants also and their brethren, that should be killed as they were, should be fulfilled." (Revelation 6:9-11)

In examining the Fifth Seal, we need to ask ourselves two questions: what is the Fifth Seal and, more importantly, *where* is the Fifth Seal?

Actually, when you read these few verses about the Fifth Seal, it is not that difficult for you to understand what this seal is talking about. Here, John saw an altar. It goes without saying that an altar is a place of sacrifice. This altar that John saw, however, is the altar of ultimate sacrifice because on this altar there were people who laid down their lives. We read that John saw the souls of them that were slain for the Word of God, and for the testimony which they held. Clearly, these people were martyrs who gave their lives for the Gospel. They were willing to die rather than deny their faith in their Lord and Savior.

Martyrdom is the wicked inflicting death upon the righteous. This comes about only because there is persecution against the Church. There is a satanic force that wants to wipe out the Church of Jesus Christ. You see, there is only *one* purpose for persecution, which is to *stop* the spread of the Gospel. Period. Persecution is not there to refine your character so that you can become more Christlike. Your character had better be Christlike already when persecution comes.

The key thing here is that the martyrs wanted God to avenge their death. So they cried out from under the altar to the Lord and asked Him when He is going to avenge them. The Lord gave them a very interesting answer. The Lord did not say that He will not take vengeance but He told them to wait for a little while. Wait for how long? Wait until *all* their fellowservants and brethren who will also be slain and killed like they were. It is pretty obvious and clear that the Fifth Seal is a time of persecution against the Church. This is what the Fifth Seal represents – a time of great persecution against the Body of Christ and that there will be many who will also die and be martyrs for Jesus Christ.

Now, at the beginning of this chapter, I stated that the two questions we need to ask ourselves are: (1) what is the Fifth Seal and (2) where is the Fifth Seal. Now that we have established that the Fifth Seal is talking about a time of great persecution, we need to know *where* this Seal is located in Matthew chapter twenty-four. We already know that the events spelled out in Revelation chapter six and Matthew chapter twenty-four are parallel. In other words, they are talking about the same thing since it is Jesus who is the One revealing the future *both* in Revelation chapter six and Matthew chapter twenty-four. It behoves us then to look at what Jesus will say next right after He finished talking about the Beginning of Sorrows, that is, the first four seals. Then we will be able to understand the **sequence of events** from the First Seal right down to the Seventh Seal.

Jesus finished talking about the Beginning of Sorrows in Matthew 24:8. Therefore let's read from verse nine onwards:

"Then shall they deliver you up to be afflicted, and shall kill you: and ye shall be hated of all nations for my name's sake. And then shall many be offended, and shall betray one another, and shall hate one another. And many false prophets shall rise, and shall deceive many. And because iniquity shall abound, the love of many shall wax cold. But he that shall endure unto the end, the same shall be saved. And this gospel of the kingdom shall be preached in all the world for a witness unto all nations; and then shall the end come. When ye therefore shall

see the abomination of desolation, spoken of by Daniel the prophet, stand in the holy place, (whoso readeth, let him understand:) Then let them which be in Judaea flee into the mountains: Let him which is on the housetop not come down to take any thing out of his house: Neither let him which is in the field return back to take his clothes. And woe unto them that are with child, and to them that give suck in those days! But pray ye that your flight be not in the winter, neither on the sabbath day: For then shall be great tribulation, such as was not since the beginning of the world to this time, no, nor ever shall be. And except those days should be shortened, there should no flesh be saved: but for the elect's sake those days shall be shortened. Then if any man shall say unto you, Lo, here is Christ, or there; believe it not. For there shall arise false Christs, and false prophets, and shall shew great signs and wonders; insomuch that, if it were possible, they shall deceive the very elect. Behold, I have told you before. Wherefore if they shall say unto you, Behold, he is in the desert; go not forth: behold, he is in the secret chambers; believe it not. For as the lightning cometh out of the east, and shineth even unto the west; so shall also the coming of the Son of man be. For wheresoever the carcase is, there will the eagles be gathered together." (Matthew 24:9-28)

Wow! Jesus was speaking the same thing as what the Fifth Seal is talking about. Just look at Matthew 24:9 alone. Jesus said they will deliver Christians up to be afflicted, and shall kill them, and Christians shall be hated of all nations for His name's sake. Therefore the entire passage of Matthew 24:9-28 is actually the Fifth Seal.

Again, do you notice an interesting parallel here? The Fifth Seal was described in a lengthier manner in Revelation 6:9-11 compared to the first four seals. Similarly, Jesus spoke about this in the greatest length and detail here in Matthew chapter twenty-four. Why? Because this period is the most critical period in the history of humankind. It is the most critical period in the history of the Jews and it is also the most critical period in the history of the Church.

You see, the Beginning of Sorrows is *sorrow upon the whole world* but the Fifth Seal is a *specific seal* and it has reference only to the Church and the Jews. It is going to be a time of travail but it is going to birth forth the return of Jesus Christ and the glorification of His Church. It is no wonder then that Jesus spoke at length and in such detail because the Fifth Seal is such an important seal as it pertains to the Church.

If Jesus called the first four seals the beginning of sorrows, then there must be a time when the sorrow increases in intensity until it reaches an end, that is, a climax. Jesus was actually talking about this climax in this passage that we read in Matthew 24:9-28, particularly from verse fifteen onwards. In verse twenty-one, Jesus said that the tribulation during this period will be great, such as was not since the beginning of the world to this time, no, nor ever shall be. This is the verse where the term "Great Tribulation" came about.

Since Jesus spoke at such length and detail here, let us spend more time looking at this passage. As mentioned earlier, this Fifth Seal will be the most critical period in the history of the nation of Israel and also for the Body of Christ. Why? Firstly, the existence of the Jewish nation will be threatened. This is one of the reasons why Jesus must come back. He must return to save the nation of Israel from total annihilation. Today we hear calls from countries like Iran for Israel to be wiped off the world map. Secondly, the Church's existence will be threatened. This is not my opinion nor my own interpretation. This is what Jesus said plainly in Matthew 24:9-10:

> *"Then they shall deliver you up to be afflicted, and shall kill you: and ye shall be hated of all nations for my name's sake. And many shall be offended, and shall betray one another, and shall hate one another." (Matthew 24:9-10)*

Don't be surprised when you, as a born-again believer, are hated by your own family members, your work colleagues, and your government. Jesus has already told us beforehand.

I hear alarm bells going off in the minds of some readers now. I hear you say, "Wait a minute, isn't the Church already raptured by this time?" You see, this is where the confusion is. Christians confuse the period of the Great Tribulation with the period of the wrath of God. But I am getting ahead of myself. We will deal with this later and we shall see things more clearly.

Jesus went on to say in verse twelve: *"And because iniquity shall abound, the love of many shall wax cold."* Persecution can come in many forms. It can be the outright killing of Christians. However, you will notice that in every nation where martyrdom occurs, a very strange phenomenon happens. The more martyrs are slain, the more Christians spring up from that place. That is why the Communist government of China has changed its tactics in its persecution against the Church. They have more or less stopped killing Christians because they realize that the more Christians they kill, the more Christians will spring up.

So Satan now uses other tactics in persecuting the Church. He now infiltrates governments, schools, universities, and even churches with godless, liberal and secular ideologies. When Christians buy into such ideologies, their love for Christ shall wax cold. Nevertheless, the killing and torturing of Christians is still Satan's favorite method of persecution.

Now, who will persecute the Church? Who will be involved? The book of Revelation talks in great detail about this. Let us realize that the Bible tells us that before Jesus comes back, there will be revealed a person with a satanic nature and a satanic power in him. The Scriptures call this man the Antichrist. The antichrist spirit is already at work in the world today through secular liberalism, communism and many other godless ideologies. However, this will lead to the manifestation of an actual person called the Antichrist. This is who Jesus was referring to in Matthew 24:15:

"When ye therefore shall see the abomination of desolation, spoken of by Daniel the prophet, stand in the holy place, (whoso readeth, let him understand)." (Matthew 24:15)

Jesus is speaking about how the Antichrist will set up his image, the abomination of desolation, in the temple of God in Jerusalem. This is described in detail by the apostle Paul in the second chapter of the second epistle to the Thessalonians:

*"Now we beseech you, brethren, by the coming of our Lord Jesus Christ, and by our gathering together unto him, That ye be not soon shaken in mind, or be troubled, neither by spirit, nor by word, nor by letter as from us, as that the **day of Christ** is at hand. Let no man deceive you by any means: **for that day shall not come**, except there come a falling away first, and that man of sin be revealed, the son of perdition; Who opposeth and exalteth himself above all that is called*

*God, or that is worshipped; so that **he as God sitteth in the temple of God**, shewing himself that he is God." (2 Thessalonians 2:1-4)*

Here Paul is writing about the same thing he wrote in 1 Thessalonians 4:15 – 5:2, the passage that we have already dealt with in chapter two of this book. Again, I want you to take note that 2 Thessalonians 2:1 tells us that the second coming of Christ and our gathering with Him takes place on ***the same day***. In verse two, Paul calls this the day of Christ. This is the same exact day as the Day of the Lord since Christ is the Lord. Paul then continues in verse three:

"Let no man deceive you by any means: for that day shall not come, except there come a falling away first, and that man of sin be revealed, the son of perdition." (2 Thessalonians 2:3)

As we have already established in chapter two of this book, the Day of the Lord is the event when Jesus comes and we are gathered (raptured) unto Him and Paul said they will all take place within the same day. Paul also mentioned that this Day will *not* come until there comes a falling away first and the man of sin, the Antichrist, is first revealed. (The "falling away" that Paul talks about is what Jesus said in Matthew 24:10-12). In other words, the second coming of our Lord Jesus Christ and the Rapture will not take place until the Antichrist first emerges onto the world scene. Simply speaking, we will meet the Antichrist! Now don't get put off and put this book down. There is nothing to be alarmed or frightened of. When we see the entire sequence of events in its entirety, we will see things clearly and be reassured. As I mentioned in the Introduction to this book, my main purpose of writing this book is to dissolve doubts and fears about end-time events. So stay with me and stay the course!

If the Church is raptured before the Antichrist comes, how then is he going to be the Antichrist when the Body of Christ is no longer around for him to *anti*? Some people say that he is going to persecute the Jews and not the Christians. They say this because they interpret Matthew 24:15-22 as referring to only the Jews. Many people read this passage and say that the persecuted people are the Jews since the Church is no longer around during the Great Tribulation. If that is the case, he should not be called the

Antichrist, but rather, "Antijew" instead! This is a misconception among many Christians but we will deal with such misconceptions in a later chapter.

THE TEMPLE IN JERUSALEM

In order for the Antichrist to set up his image in the Holy Place, which the Bible calls the abomination of desolation, the temple of God will *first* have to be rebuilt in Jerusalem. Right now, there is no Jewish temple. The site where God's temple is supposed to sit on is situated right next to the Al-Aqsa mosque, which is located on the Temple Mount. It is the third most important mosque to the Muslims. Many people say that the third temple of God will never be rebuilt, because for it to be rebuilt, nothing short of a political earthquake will have to occur, or perhaps even a literal earthquake. But there is *no* need to concern ourselves as to *how* the third temple is going to be rebuilt. With man, it is impossible but with God, all things are possible. It is not only possible, it *will* be rebuilt. We are not here to debate the exact site of where the third temple shall be erected, but rebuilt it will be. It is already written in God's Word, which is forever settled in heaven, and will certainly come to pass no matter what. Therefore, the moment we see the rebuilding of the Jewish temple of God in Jerusalem, we can be assured that the Fifth Seal is well and truly opened!

I believe that we are now in the initial stages of the opening of the Fifth Seal. Many Christians have already been killed for their faith over the centuries but the persecution and the killing is intensifying. Just take the Islamic State (ISIL) for example. They have systematically tortured and killed thousands of Iraqi Christians (especially in Mosul) in all sorts of unimaginably brutal ways. To these Christians, the Fifth Seal is very real for them. To these Iraqi believers, it is great tribulation for them. What tribulation can be greater than being tortured and killed? How then can we say that the Church will no longer be around before the Great Tribulation? If the Body of Christ is to be raptured before the Great Tribulation, how can these precious Christians in Iraq and many other parts of the world be tortured and killed? Why should the rest of us be exempted and not them? They are our brethren in the faith! What we are witnessing is the beginning and the persecution will grow in intensity until the Fifth Seal has come to pass in its entirety.

THE REIGN OF THE ANTICHRIST

The stage is being set for the Scriptures to be fulfilled and the temple will eventually be rebuilt in Jerusalem. When the Antichrist emerges, he will set up his image inside it and he will make the Jews acknowledge that he is their messiah that has come. He will also perform signs and wonders by the power and authority of Satan:

"Even him, whose coming is after the working of Satan with all power and signs and lying wonders." (2 Thessalonians 2:9)

So he will deceive the Jews and even the world into believing him as the messiah because of the miracles he can do. Many people will be deceived by the deceptive power of the Antichrist and will acknowledge him as the messiah.

"And it was given unto him to make war with the saints, and to overcome them: and power was given him over all kindreds, and tongues, and nations." (Revelation 13:7)

However, Christians have already been forewarned by the Scriptures and we will not fall into his deception. Many of us will know him when he comes and we will not worship him. There is no need for us to speculate whether it is this person or that person who is going to turn out to be the Antichrist. So many articles have been written and videos have been uploaded onto various social media platforms to claim that this individual or that individual will become the Antichrist. There is no need for us to waste our time and energy wondering who he is; but we will have a more in-depth look at the Antichrist person in a later chapter. One thing for certain is that the Antichrist will have an intense hatred for Israel and the Body of Christ. Therefore when the Antichrist emerges on the world scene, we ***will*** know. So don't sweat it!

There will arise a great persecution against the Body of Christ. Why? Firstly, he will come against us because we refuse to worship his image.

*"And all that dwell upon the earth shall worship him, **whose names are not written** in the book of life of the Lamb slain from the foundation of the world." (Revelation 13:8)*

If our names are written in the Lamb's book of life, it means that we are born again and we belong to Him and we know His voice. We will therefore have the discernment and we will not bow and worship the Antichrist's image, just like Shadrach, Meschach and Abednego refused to bow down before the image of king Nebuchadnezzar (see Daniel chapter three). The image of the Antichrist is not going to be just a physical statue in the temple in Jerusalem. He will attempt to cause his virtual image to pervade almost every home and impose it on all strata of society, monitoring everyone to see whether we worship his image or not. If this book was written in the 1980s or the 1990s, it would have been rather difficult to envisage such a scenario. Now with the advent of Artificial Intelligence, 5G technology and the Internet of Things we are getting very close. The digital and information technology that we cannot live without today, coupled with the use of big data, are actually grooming and conditioning society for this very purpose.

Let me quote a report released by Open Doors USA on January 15, 2020:

> *"In China (No. 23), where there are an estimated 97 million Christians, persecution against Christians has taken a technological turn. A recent report cited by CNBC estimates there are approximately 415 million surveillance cameras in China, a number only expected to grow in coming years. China has also developed widespread facial recognition software and established laws requiring facial scans to purchase a phone. When taken together, these two technological advances mean the government can track individuals like never before. China is also rolling out a country-wide Social Credit System (SCS) by which authorities plan to reward "good" citizenship and punish "bad." Already, one community has reportedly decided to add penalties for those who "illegally spread Christianity." It's easy to see how surveillance technology could be used in tandem with the SCS to make everyday life very difficult for anyone the Chinese government deems insufficiently "Chinese" – including Christians.*

Similarly, in India (No. 10), the government plans to introduce a national facial recognition system. There were at least 447 verified incidents of violence and hate crimes against Christians in India in the 2020 World Watch List reporting period. There is fear that more tracking could increase these attacks."

The second reason that there will arise a great persecution against the Church is that we will not take his mark on our hand or our forehead.

"And he causeth all, both small and great, rich and poor, free and bond, to receive a mark in their right hand, or in their foreheads: And that no man might buy or sell, save he that had the mark, or the name of the beast, or the number of his name. Here is wisdom. Let him that hath understanding count the number of the beast: for it is the number of a man; and his number is Six hundred threescore and six." (Revelation 13:16-18)

What is this mark that the Antichrist will impose on people worldwide? Some say that it is going to be a microchip. It could very well be, but again, let's not sweat over what form it will take. We have the Holy Spirit within us who will lead us and tell us what to do when the time comes. But I would like to point out once again that society is being conditioned to accept the mark of the beast with the advancement of technology. Only just two centuries ago, the medium of exchange for selling and buying was gold or silver. Since carrying gold or silver around was not convenient, people came up with banknotes which value were backed up by the gold or silver they own. However, people still found it was not convenient to carry a huge stash of banknotes around, so check-writing was introduced. Still, people found issuing checks to be a hassle, so the credit card was introduced. Now you don't even have to bring along your credit or debit card. All you need to do is register your credit card with your cellphone and flash your cellphone at the checkout counter. Soon, people will find carrying a cellphone to be inconvenient. So you end up with a microchip (or whatever form it takes) in your hand or forehead, which you will never forget to bring along! With the advent of Central Bank Digital Currency (CBDC), the world is speeding along towards the economic system of the beast. I am bringing all this out to show how the world is being groomed and conditioned to readily accept the mark of the beast.

Because we have been forewarned by the Bible, we will boycott the Antichrist's economic system. The Body of Christ will then suffer his wrath. We will not be able to buy or sell anything. We will not be able to pay for our utility bills, fuel, or anything at all. Sounds too far-fetched? Well, not too long ago, people in many parts of the world were not able to enter supermarkets or restaurants to buy groceries or food unless they could show some sort of proof that they had been vaccinated against Covid-19. And most folks quietly complied. Think about that for a moment. That was just a dry-run. When the real thing comes, believers will face such a terrible worldwide persecution that Jesus said:

*"And except those days should be shortened, there should no flesh be saved: but for the **elect's sake** those days shall be shortened." (Matthew 24:22)*

Shortened to how long? It is often mentioned as "time, times, and half a time" (Daniel 12:7). In other passages, it is mentioned as forty-two months (Revelation 11:2 and Revelation 13:5). So the period of the Great Tribulation will last three and a half years. Who is the elect? The Body of Christ!

I would like to reiterate that I am not being a fear-monger here. I am not an alarmist. I am merely laying out what Jesus has so clearly and plainly said in the Bible so that we will be well prepared and not caught off-guard. Remember, Jesus spent much more time talking about the Fifth Seal than the other seals. This means we had better pay attention. We are, without doubt, witnessing the initial stages of the opening of the Fifth Seal. The time span for this seal to be fully opened remains to be seen. However, we are not here to determine the time span, but the time sequence of events.

Chapter 6

OPENING OF THE SIXTH SEAL

THE SIXTH SEAL

*"And I beheld when he had opened the sixth seal, and, lo, there was a great earthquake; and **the sun became black as sackcloth of hair, and the moon became as blood; And the stars of heaven fell unto the earth**, even as a fig tree casteth her untimely figs, when she is shaken of a mighty wind. And the heaven departed as a scroll when it is rolled together; and every mountain and island were moved out of their places. And the kings of the earth, and the great men, and the rich men, and the chief captains, and the mighty men, and every bondman, and every free man, hid themselves in the dens and in the rocks of the mountains; And said to the mountains and rocks, Fall on us, and hide us from the face of him that sitteth on the throne, and from the wrath of the Lamb: For the great day of his wrath is come; and who shall be able to stand?" (Revelation 6:12-17)*

We have finally arrived at the Sixth Seal. This is it – the climax. Look at verse twelve. It says that the sun became black as sackcloth of hair, and the moon became as blood, and the stars of heaven fell unto the earth. Now, look at Matthew 24:29-30:

*"Immediately after the tribulation of those days shall **the sun be darkened, and the moon shall not give her light, and the stars shall fall from heaven**, and the powers of the heavens shall be shaken: And then shall appear the sign of the Son of man in heaven: and then shall all the tribes of the earth mourn, and they shall see the Son of man coming in the clouds of heaven with power and great glory." (Matthew 24:29-30)*

Look at what Jesus said in verse twenty-nine. It is exactly the same as verse twelve of Revelation chapter six! I don't know about you, but I still get awed every time I read these two passages of Scriptures together.

So when does this event take place? Jesus said that it shall occur *"immediately after the tribulation of those days"*. That's right, the Blackout described in the Sixth Seal shall take place immediately after the Great Tribulation, the Fifth Seal. That's the time sequence there. It's really elementary.

What happens next? Well, in Matthew 24:30, Jesus said that the sign of the Son of man shall appear in heaven and that all the tribes (peoples) of the earth shall see the Son of man coming in the clouds of heaven with power and great glory. Against the backdrop of this cosmic blackout, the Lord Jesus Christ returns in all His glory and splendour!

Remember what we read in chapter two of this book? Allow me to mention it here again.

"The sun shall be turned into darkness, and the moon into blood, before the great and terrible day of the Lord come." (Joel 2:31)

"Multitudes, multitudes in the valley of decision: for the day of the Lord is near in the valley of decision. The sun and the moon shall be darkened, and the stars shall withdraw their shining." (Joel 3:14-15)

Can you see it now? Can you see how everything ties up together? It is the Day of the Lord! The day that you and I have been waiting and longing for. The day that Jesus comes back for His beloved Bride, holy and blameless. If you want to put the book down and run around the room and shout a bit, go ahead! Because it is Rapture time!

Let's go back to the book of First Thessalonians to remind ourselves what happens on the Day of the Lord:

"For the Lord himself shall descend from heaven with a shout, with the voice of the archangel, and with the trump of God: and the dead in Christ shall rise first: Then we which are alive and remain shall be caught up together with them in the clouds, to meet the Lord in the air: and so shall we ever be with the Lord.

Wherefore comfort one another with these words. But of the times and the seasons, brethren, ye have no need that I write unto you. For yourselves know perfectly that the day of the Lord so cometh as a thief in the night." (1 Thessalonians 4:16-5:2)

Is not the above passage consistent with what Jesus said in Matthew 24:30-31? Have a look at it again:

"And then shall appear the sign of the Son of man in heaven: and then shall all the tribes of the earth mourn, and they shall see the Son of man coming in the clouds of heaven with power and great glory. And he shall send his angels with a great sound of a trumpet, and they shall gather together his elect from the four winds, from one end of heaven to the other." (Matthew 24:30-31)

Both Paul and Jesus are talking about the same thing in the above passages. Jesus describes the rapture of the Church as sending His angels to gather together His elect from the four winds, from one end of heaven to the other. In other words, the Rapture occurs worldwide, wherever you, as a born-again believer, are located. You don't have to go to a special place to get raptured. And no born-again believer who has put his or her faith in the Lord Jesus Christ and His finished redemptive work of the cross will be left behind. "Sure," you say, "how about Christians who have backslidden?" Well, if a believer is truly in a backslidden state, he or she would have easily been deceived by the Antichrist or they would have succumbed to the pressure of receiving the mark of the beast and worshipping his image. Having taken the mark of the beast, he or she then would have forfeited his or her salvation and thus not be raptured. It's as simple as that. However, I want to encourage every believer not to underestimate the power of the Holy Spirit whom we have been sealed with to preserve us holy and blameless until the Day of the Lord (1 Corinthians 1:8). We need to remember that greater is He that is in us than he that is in the world (1 John 4:4)!

THE TWO RUNS

One of the fascinating discoveries, as we study the second coming of Jesus Christ, is the interesting placement of events that come **before** and

after the Blackout in the heavens (the Sixth Seal). The arrangement gives us a series of two runs, one before the Blackout and one after the Blackout.

We saw that the Fifth Seal is the period of persecution and martyrdom during the reign of the Antichrist for three and a half years. In identifying this man of sin, Jesus referred to Daniel's prophecy concerning the abomination of desolation, which is the image of the Antichrist, standing in the holy place. We will look at the warning given by Jesus in Matthew chapter twenty-four to see the first run.

THE FIRST RUN

"When ye therefore shall see the abomination of desolation, spoken of by Daniel the prophet, stand in the holy place, (whoso readeth, let him understand:) Then let them which be in Judaea flee into the mountains: Let him which is on the housetop not come down to take any thing out of his house: Neither let him which is in the field return back to take his clothes. And woe unto them that are with child, and to them that give suck in those days! But pray ye that your flight be not in the winter, neither on the sabbath day: For then shall be great tribulation, such as was not since the beginning of the world to this time, no, nor ever shall be. And except those days should be shortened, there should no flesh be saved: but for the elect's sake those days shall be shortened." (Matthew 24:15-22)

Jesus said that when we see the abomination of desolation standing in the holy place (the Jewish temple of God), then those who are in Judea should flee to the mountains. Why? Firstly, we need to identify the location carefully. Judea is where Jerusalem is located and Jerusalem is where the holy place is. Being in Judea would therefore mean being closest to where the abomination of desolation is. Jesus advocates running to the mountain because there is danger. The danger arises from the Antichrist imposing the worship of his image. Revelation 13:15 tells us that those who refuse to worship that image will be killed. In order to avoid the wrath of the Antichrist against those who refuse to worship his image, Jesus said we should run to the mountains. The mountains are the place of safety because of the forest canopy and vegetation which will provide a suitable place to hide. All Christians and God-fearing Jews will therefore run and hide. This is the **first run**.

The urgency of fleeing is emphasized by Jesus when He said that if someone is on the housetop, he should not take anything out of his house. The temptation of taking things we treasure will cost us valuable time needed to escape and the carrying of things with us will impede our haste. Therefore, Jesus also said that if we are in the field we should not return and we should pray that our flight would not be in the winter for the simple reason that winter time is not conducive for fleeing, and neither is the burden of carrying and looking after a very young child. All this means that the moment the Antichrist is revealed we must not delay but immediately go into hiding.

Jesus is basically saying that we should run and hide. Jesus therefore does not advocate bravado and confrontation with the Antichrist and his agents. He advocates concealment and not arrest. This does not mean denying our Lord but surviving during this period to avoid capture. However, if we are caught and apprehended, there is no room for compromise and we must be ready to pledge our allegiance to the Lamb and die for the faith.

In Matthew 10:28, Jesus encouraged us with these words:

"And fear not them which kill the body, but are not able to kill the soul: but rather fear Him which is able to destroy both soul and body in hell." (Matthew 10:28)

Once we are arrested, we cannot compromise so as to avoid the wrath of the Antichrist. To compromise and to accept his mark or worship his image will mean we will not escape the wrath of God:

"And the third angel followed them, saying with a loud voice, If any man worship the beast and his image, and receive his mark in his forehead, or in his hand, The same shall drink of the wine of the wrath of God, which is poured out without mixture into the cup of his indignation; and he shall be tormented with fire and brimstone in the presence of the holy angels, and in the presence of the Lamb: And the smoke of their torment ascendeth up for ever and ever: and they have no rest day nor night, who worship the beast and his image, and whosoever receiveth the mark of his name." (Revelation 14:9-11)

Why escape the wrath of the Antichrist and later fall into the wrath of God? The very next verse encourages us with these words:

"Here is the patience of the saints: here are they that keep the commandments of God, and the faith of Jesus." (Revelation 14:12)

Here is another piece of Scriptural evidence that we, the saints of God, are still around during the reign of the Antichrist. The word *patience* in the Greek is the word *hupomone*. It is defined as "steadfastness, constancy, endurance – in the NT the characteristic of a man who is not swerved from his deliberate purpose and his loyalty to faith and piety by even the greatest trials and sufferings" (Thayer). In other words, during the time of the Antichrist, our steadfastness, constancy, and endurance must shine through. Again, there is no need to sweat it, as these attributes are already inside us when we became born again by the Spirit of God.

Look at the next verse:

"And I heard a voice from heaven saying unto me, Write, Blessed are the dead which die in the Lord from henceforth: Yea, saith the Spirit, that they may rest from their labours; and their works do follow them." (Revelation 14:13)

Death is a blessing if we die in the Lord. Don't misunderstand me – I am not talking about premature death due to sickness, disease or accidents. Here, the verse is talking about dying for the faith because we refuse to worship the Antichrist or take his mark. In fact, that ought to be the only reason if we are to die prematurely – martyrdom. Otherwise, we ought to live out the full lifespan of man. The Lord Jesus Christ has paid in full the price for the healing of our physical bodies (see Isaiah 53:3-5 and Matthew 8:17) so healing belongs to us whenever we are confronted with sickness and disease.

This first run will end when the Blackout takes place after the three and a half years reign of the Antichrist. Jesus will then return in power and glory, and at His return, **sinners** will run and hide!

THE SECOND RUN

Let us refer to the Sixth Seal in Revelation 6:12-17 again:

"And I beheld when he had opened the sixth seal, and, lo, there was a great earthquake; and the sun became black as sackcloth of hair, and the moon became as blood; And the stars of heaven fell unto the earth, even as a fig tree casteth her

untimely figs, when she is shaken of a mighty wind. And the heaven departed as a scroll when it is rolled together; and every mountain and island were moved out of their places. ***And the kings of the earth, and the great men, and the rich men, and the chief captains, and the mighty men, and every bondman, and every free man, hid themselves in the dens and in the rocks of the mountains; And said to the mountains and rocks, Fall on us, and hide us from the face of him that sitteth on the throne, and from the wrath of the Lamb: For the great day of his wrath is come; and who shall be able to stand?"*** *(Revelation 6:12-17)*

We now know that the Blackout will usher in the return of our Lord and Savior, Jesus Christ. Men and women, both small and great, every world leader, will call on the mountains and rocks to fall on them and hide them from the face of Jesus sitting on the throne. They will be filled with so much terror that they would rather be crushed by the mountains and rocks than see the glorious face of the Lamb upon the throne. Why? The answer is obvious for the great day of God's wrath has come. We have already seen that this is the Day of the Lord. You see, the Day of the Lord is a day of great rejoicing, jubilation and triumph for all Christians who have endured to the very end; but it is a day of great terror and mourning for everyone who has rejected the Gospel of Jesus during their lifetime. This is the **second run**.

The Blackout in the heavens is therefore a very important event – it demarcates two periods, separating the two wraths and the two runs. In other words, the Blackout demarcates two major periods: the Great Tribulation and the great and terrible Day of the Lord.

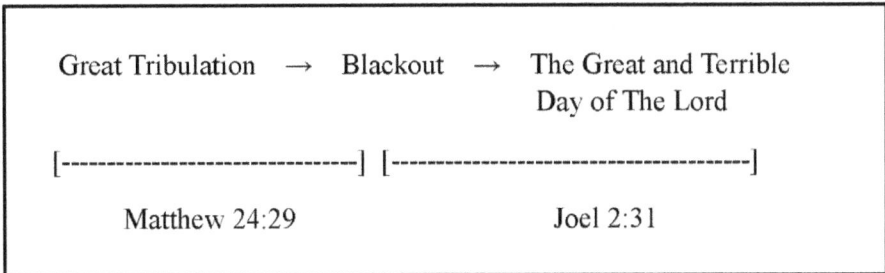

Great Tribulation   →   Blackout   →   The Great and Terrible Day of The Lord

[-----------------------------] [--------------------------------------]

Matthew 24:29   Joel 2:31

The Blackout divides two wraths – that of the Antichrist and that of Christ.

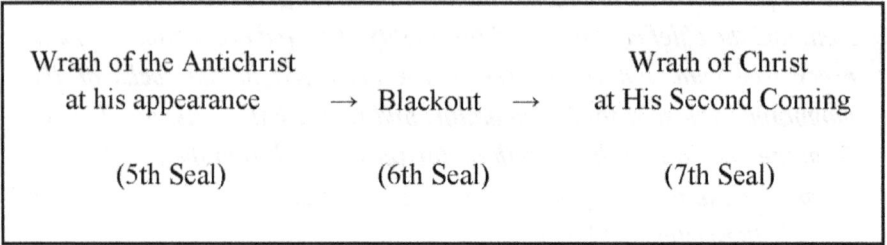

Wrath of the Antichrist at his appearance	→ Blackout →	Wrath of Christ at His Second Coming
(5th Seal)	(6th Seal)	(7th Seal)

The Blackout therefore separates two runs – the first run by the saints and the second run by sinners.

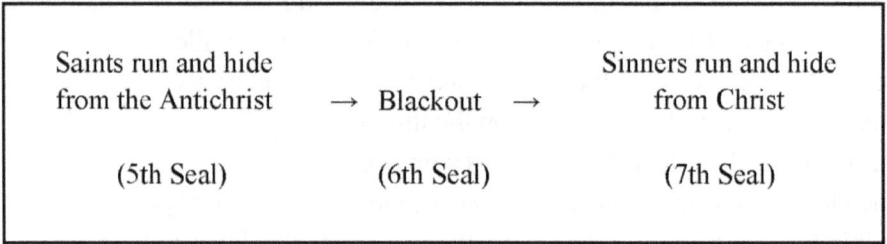

Saints run and hide from the Antichrist	→ Blackout →	Sinners run and hide from Christ
(5th Seal)	(6th Seal)	(7th Seal)

Since the Blackout is the Sixth Seal in the book of Revelation and it is followed by the wrath of God, we can safely conclude that the Seventh Seal is the wrath of God. We shall look at this in the next chapter. We want to end this chapter with an important question though: which run will you participate in? The first run or the second run?

Chapter 7

OPENING OF THE SEVENTH SEAL

THE SEVENTH SEAL – THE WRATH OF GOD

In the sixth chapter of Revelation, we have seen that the Sixth Seal speaks of a Blackout that is to take place in the heavens. This Blackout is explained in Joel 2:31 as a sign that the Day of the Lord has come. Just before Jesus returns, the whole sky shall be plunged into total darkness. The heavens will then open and our Lord will be revealed in the clouds in power and great glory. We will then know that the Day of the Lord has finally come (it is going to be fun to see how the news channels report on this).

"For the great day of His wrath is come and who shall be able to stand?" (Revelation 6:17)

Revelation 6:17 tells us that when Jesus comes, every person who does not know Him will be terrified of even looking at Him and all will run and hide. This is further corroborated by the prophet Isaiah:

*"Howl ye; for **the day of the LORD** is at hand; it shall come as a destruction from the Almighty. Therefore shall all hands be faint, and every man's heart shall melt: And they shall be afraid: pangs and sorrows shall take hold of them; they shall be in pain as a woman that travaileth: they shall be amazed one at another; their faces shall be as flames. Behold, **the day of the LORD cometh**, cruel both with wrath and fierce anger, to lay the land desolate: and he shall destroy the sinners thereof out of it. For **the stars of heaven and the constellations thereof shall not give their light: the sun shall be darkened in his going forth, and the moon shall not cause her light to shine."* (Isaiah 13:6-10)*

See the consistency of the Bible regarding the Day of the Lord? Here we read that on the Day of the Lord, the wrath of God shall be poured out upon the sinners and the wicked. Isaiah 13:10 and the Sixth Seal of Revelation chapter six are really saying the same thing. It follows that the Seventh Seal described in Revelation chapters eight, nine and eleven is the pouring out of the wrath of God upon the wicked. But before chapter eight, we read in chapter seven that the Church is raptured. Therefore we will escape the wrath of God.

> *"After this I beheld, and, lo, a great multitude, which no man could number, of all nations, and kindreds, and people, and tongues, stood before the throne, and before the Lamb, clothed with white robes, and palms in their hands." (Revelation 7:9)*

We are thus able to conclude that after Jesus Christ returns in power and great glory (Revelation chapter six), we will see the Church standing before the throne (Revelation chapter seven). This agrees with the fourth chapter of First Thessalonians (which we are now already familiar with) which states that when Jesus comes, the dead in Christ will rise, and the rest of us who are still alive, will be caught up together with them to meet the Lord in the air. So the entire Body of Christ will be raptured and will stand before the throne of God.

The entire sequence of the events is as follows as shown in the graphic on the next page:

1st Seal DECEPTION	Rev 6:1-2 Matt 24:4-5
2nd Seal WAR	Rev 6:3-4 Matt 24:6-7
3rd Seal FAMINE	Rev 6:5-6 Matt 24:7
4th Seal DEATH	Rev 6:7-8 Matt 24:7
5th Seal GREAT TRIBULATION	Rev 6:9-11 Matt 24:9-21
6th Seal BLACKOUT	Rev 6:12-13 Matt 24:29
THE DAY OF THE LORD	1 Thess 4:15-5:2 Matt 24:30-31 Joel 2:31
7th Seal WRATH OF GOD	Rev 6:14-17 Isa 13:6-10

IS THE GREAT TRIBULATION THE WRATH OF GOD?

This is the question on everyone's mind. The Fifth Seal is the time of the Great Tribulation, the Sixth Seal is the Blackout in the heavens and the Seventh Seal is the pouring out of the wrath of God. There are many who would posit that chapters five to eighteen of the book of Revelation are all talking about the Great Tribulation period. This is the point where we have gone wrong. The important thing to realize is that the moment the Blackout takes place, the Great Tribulation is all over. You see, the Blackout takes place in Revelation 6:12-13. Now then, Matthew 24:29 says that the Blackout happens right after the Great Tribulation. Simple logic then tells us that since the Blackout is after the Great Tribulation, the latter must be before Revelation 6:12-13. Hence chapters five to eighteen cannot be the Great

Tribulation! Jesus comes back right after the Blackout. The moment Jesus comes, the Church is raptured and then the wrath of God is poured out.

It is vital that we **do not confuse** the Great Tribulation with the wrath of God. If you cannot differentiate between the two, you will say that the Church must be raptured before the Tribulation. Why? Because if you read about the Seventh Seal, you will see the awesome terror of God's wrath and wonder how God could ever allow His beloved bride to go through it all. That is why so many preachers and Christians are so fearful of the Great Tribulation, thinking that it also includes the wrath of God. But, as we have seen, the Scriptures are very clear: before the Seventh Seal, the Body of Christ would already have been raptured. HalleluYah!

As we have earlier seen, after the Great Tribulation the sun will be darkened, the moon will no longer give its light and then will appear the sign of the Son of Man in heaven. He will send His angels with a great sound of the trumpet and will gather His elect from the four winds. After the Church is caught up in a place of safety with the Lord, the Seventh Seal is opened whereupon God will pour out His wrath on the wicked as detailed in Revelation chapter eight.

"And when he had opened the seventh seal, there was silence in heaven about the space of half an hour. And I saw the seven angels which stood before God; and to them were given seven trumpets." (Revelation 8:1-2)

THE LAW OF DOUBLE MENTION

In Revelation chapter eight, we read about the pouring out of the wrath of God on the wicked and all those who rejected the Gospel. Now, if we look at Revelation chapter sixteen, we will find another passage that talks about the wrath of God.

"And I heard a great voice out of the temple saying to the seven angels, Go your ways, and pour out the vials of the wrath of God upon the earth." (Revelation 16:1)

Again we have seven angels, but this time, instead of trumpets, they have vials (or bowls) full of the wrath of God. Now, the question is this – are there two periods of the wrath of God or is there only one?

If you look through the Bible, you will find that there is only one time which is called the wrath of God and this is when Jesus Christ returns on the Day of the Lord. We have already established that the Day of the Lord is a day of wrath. Why then does the book of Revelation have two separate sections about the wrath of God? In answering this question, we will discover an important key in understanding the book of Revelation. To unearth the key, let us go back to an Old Testament passage to see and understand a very important principle of Bible prophecy.

Let us look at Genesis chapter forty-one and the story of Joseph interpreting the dream of Pharaoh. God gave Pharaoh two dreams. In the first one, Pharaoh dreamt of seven fat cows by a river and seven lean cows feeding in a meadow. The cows were on opposite sides of the river and Pharaoh saw the fat ones being eaten up by the scrawny ones. In the second dream, Pharaoh saw seven ears of corn that were fat and fleshy and another seven that were very thin and blasted. He also saw the seven fat ears being eaten up by the lean ones.

If you were Pharaoh, you would expect two interpretations because you had two dreams. But when Joseph came before Pharaoh, he told Pharaoh that the dreams were, in fact, the same.

*"And Joseph said unto Pharaoh, **The dream of Pharaoh is one**: God hath shewed Pharaoh what he is about to do." (Genesis 41:25)*

If the two dreams both speak of the same thing, why then did God double it? The answer is found in verse thirty-two:

*"And for that the dream was **doubled** unto Pharaoh twice; it is because the thing is established by God, and God will shortly bring it to pass." (Genesis 41:32)*

What then is the purpose of doubling the dream? It is to establish the fact. The first is a "yea" and the second an "amen". It is to establish and confirm what God has revealed. The whole purpose of God repeating Pharaoh's dream was to let him know that the matter has been established and will surely come to pass. From here we have a very simple law of prophecy: when God speaks through prophecy, He will always give a confirmation. The second is to confirm the fact of the first. This is called **the law of double mention**.

Now that we understand the principle of double mention, we can see that there cannot be two periods when God pours out His wrath. The seven trumpets and the seven vials are actually the same. Revelation chapter six already says that the Day of His wrath has come and after this we have the Seventh Seal which details the seven trumpets of wrath. Then in chapter sixteen, we have the seven vials of wrath. We can therefore conclude that **the seven trumpets and the seven vials are one and the same except that the symbols were changed**, very much like the two dreams of Joseph.

In the first description of the wrath of God, the symbol used is the trumpet. In the second description, the symbol used is the vial. Both these symbols were chosen because they are very appropriate. Firstly, the trumpet is a very apt symbol for anger. We know that when a person is angry, he blasts out! Likewise, the trumpet blasts out sound. The Day of the Lord is when God will show His anger and He will blast it out upon the wicked.

Secondly, we have the bowls or vials. The vial is also a very suitable symbol for anger and wrath. The content inside a vial is meant to be poured out. Similarly, anger is kept inside a person until it can no longer be contained and is poured out one day. Revelation chapter sixteen speaks about the cup of God's wrath:

> *"And the great city was divided into three parts, and the cities of the nations fell: and great Babylon came in remembrance before God, to give unto her **the cup of the wine of the fierceness of his wrath**." (Revelation 16:19)*

So there is a cup of wrath and it is being filled with the wrath of God. The time has not come for the pouring out of God's judgment but when Jesus Christ returns, the door of grace will be closed and God will pour forth His wrath on sinners. That is why God seems to be painfully slow in bringing about justice on the wicked who have committed heinous, unspeakable acts. It seems that the wicked, the corrupt, murderers, schemers, liars, manipulators can get away with it with impunity. It appears that those who speak up and stand up for justice and righteousness are often shut up and persecuted while evil men are celebrated by the world. It is because God is longsuffering and is not willing that any person should perish but come to the saving knowledge of Jesus Christ. We must realise that the same grace that has been extended to you and me by God is also extended to the unrighteous. But when the Day of the Lord arrives, there will be no more opportunity for anyone to repent and ask for forgiveness because Jesus will not be coming back as the Lamb of God but as the King of kings and Lord of lords. On that Day, everyone who thought that he or she could get away with it will drink the cup of the wine of the fierceness of His fury!

Hence from Genesis chapter forty-one we get the key to understand the book of Revelation. Revelation is actually a doubly-mentioned book. We have events running all the way down to chapter eleven where the end of the world is recorded. The time sequence stops in chapter eleven and from chapter twelve onward, we have a re-run of all the previous events. In the re-run, certain key events and personalities have been highlighted and described in greater detail.

Here is another table for you to have a better picture of the template of events:

Revelation 1	Introductory
Revelation 2-3	Warning and Exhortation
Revelation 4	John taken up to Heaven
Revelation 5	Presentation of the Book with the Seven Seals
Revelation 6	Events leading to the Second Coming of Christ
Revelation 7	The Rapture
Revelation 8, 9, 11	The Pouring Out of God's Wrath

So the sequence actually runs from chapters six to eleven and it gives the **macroscopic view** of the future. However, from chapter twelve onwards, we have the highlights and details so we 'zoom' in to have a **microscopic view**. This is what the rest of the book of Revelation is – the highlighting of details which run in sequence until the end, to the time when Jesus establishes His eternal kingdom. Chapters twenty-one and twenty-two usher us into eternity.

As Revelation is a doubly-mentioned book, we see Jesus coming in both chapters six and fourteen. We also have the 144,000 in both chapters seven and fourteen. We have the wrath of God in chapters eight, nine and eleven and again in chapter sixteen. Everything has been repeated. Six such repetitions are listed below:

EVENT	FIRST MENTION	SECOND MENTION
Great Tribulation	Chapter 6:9-11	Chapters 12 and 13
Second Coming of Jesus	Chapter 6:14-17	Chapter 14:14
Sealing of the "144,000"	Chapter 7:2-4	Chapter 14:1
Rapture	Chapter 7:9-10	Chapter 14:15-16
Preparation for the Wrath of God	Chapter 8:1-6	Chapter 15
The Wrath of God	Chapter 8:7 – 9:21 Chapter 11:15-19	Chapter 16

Chapter 8

THE SEVEN TRUMPETS

AND

SEVEN VIALS

In this chapter, we shall briefly compare each of the trumpets with the vials to give us a detailed understanding of the wrath of God. You may be thinking why this would concern us since the Body of Christ has already been raptured. Well, the Word of God is the revealed will of God. If God has put it in His Word, then He has meant it for us to read and understand it. If He did not want us to know about it, He would not have included all these chapters about the wrath of God. In any case, it makes us all that much more thankful and appreciative to know that we have been saved and redeemed from the awesome terror of His wrath. It also informs us of what awaits everyone who has been too stubborn and proud to receive Jesus Christ as their Lord and Redeemer!

THE FIRST TRUMPET AND VIAL

"The first angel sounded, and there followed hail and fire mingled with blood, and they were cast upon the earth: and the third part of trees was burnt up, and all green grass was burnt up." (Revelation 8:7)

"And the first went, and poured out his vial upon the earth; and there fell a noisome and grievous sore upon the men which had the mark of the beast, and upon them which worshipped his image." (Revelation 16:2)

In comparing the first trumpet with the first vial, let us identify their common denominator. Looking at the two passages, the common phrase is *"upon the earth"*. Revelation 8:7 tells us that hail and fire were cast upon the earth while Revelation 16:2 speaks of a noisome and grievous sore that fell upon men.

Those who have experienced a hailstorm can testify that when hail fall from the sky, it produces a very noisy roar. Thus the "hail" in Revelation 8:7 and the "noisome" element in Revelation 16:2 both point to the same thing. Then we see "fire mingled with blood" and "grievous sore", leading us to conclude that men were burnt. When Revelation 8:7 says that a third of the trees and all green grass were burnt up, it has both a literal and symbolic meaning. Symbolically, the "trees" and "grass" refer to men. We can see this very clearly in Psalm 1:1-3:

> *"Blessed is the man that walketh not in the counsel of the ungodly, nor standeth in the way of sinners, nor sitteth in the seat of the scornful. But his delight is in the law of the LORD; and in his law doth he meditate day and night. And he shall be like a tree planted by the rivers of water, that bringeth forth his fruit in his season; his leaf also shall not wither; and whatsoever he doeth shall prosper." (Psalm1:1-3)*

In Isaiah chapter forty, we see that grass also symbolises humans:

> *"The voice said, Cry. And he said, What shall I cry?* **All flesh is grass**, *and all the goodliness thereof is as the flower of the field: The grass withereth, the flower fadeth: because the spirit of the LORD bloweth upon it:* **surely the people is grass**.*" (Isaiah 40:6-7)*

Thus we see that those who have the mark of the beast and worshipped his image in Revelation 16:2 and the third of the trees and all the grass in Revelation 8:7 are the same. Chapter sixteen uses plain words while chapter eight uses symbols but essentially the first trumpet is the same as the first vial.

	Revelation 8:7	Revelation 16:2
Common Denominator	"Upon the earth"	"Upon the earth"
Similar Event	The third part of trees was burnt up, and all green grass was burnt up ("Trees" and "grass" symbolise men)	There fell a noisome and grievous sore upon the men which had the mark of the beast, and upon them which worshipped his image

THE SECOND TRUMPET AND VIAL

*"And the second angel sounded, and as it were a great mountain burning with fire was cast **into the sea**: and **the third part of the sea became blood**; And the third part of the creatures which were in the sea, and had life, died; and the third part of the ships were destroyed." (Revelation 8:8-9)*

*"And the second angel poured out his vial **upon the sea**; and **it became as the blood** of a dead man: and every living soul died in the sea." (Revelation 16:3)*

In Revelation 8:8, we see that the second trumpet caused something like a mountain to fall into the sea while in Revelation 16:3, the content of second bowl was also poured upon the sea. The second trumpet and vial remind us of one of the ten plagues of Moses in Egypt where the river was turned to blood. So the second wrath of God speaks of the oceans and seas turning to blood.

	Revelation 8:8-9	Revelation 16:3
Common Denominator	"Into the sea"	"Upon the sea"
Similar Event	The sea became blood	The sea became as the blood of a dead man

THE THIRD TRUMPET AND VIAL

*"And the third angel sounded, and there fell a great star from heaven, burning as it were a lamp, and it fell upon **the third part of the rivers, and upon the fountains of waters;** And the name of the star is called Wormwood: and the third part of the waters became wormwood; and many men died of the waters, because **they were made bitter.**" (Revelation 8:10-11)*

*"And the third angel poured out his vial **upon the rivers and fountains of waters; and they became blood.** And I heard the angel of the waters say, Thou art righteous, O Lord, which art, and wast, and shalt be, because thou hast judged thus. For they have shed the blood of saints and prophets, and thou hast given them blood to drink; for they are worthy. And I heard another out of the altar say, Even so, Lord God Almighty, true and righteous are thy judgments." (Revelation 16:4-7)*

The third trumpet tells us that the water has become wormwood or bitter while the third bowl describes the waters as having become blood. The conclusion is, however, the same – men could not drink water that has become bitter or has turned to blood. The third judgment upon the world is that rivers and fountains will become undrinkable and humans will die from drinking it.

	Revelation 8:10-11	Revelation 16:4-7
Common Denominator	"Upon…the rivers, and upon the fountains of waters"	"Upon the rivers and fountains of waters"
Similar Event	The waters became bitter (undrinkable)	The waters became blood (undrinkable)

THE FOURTH TRUMPET AND VIAL

*"And the fourth angel sounded, and the third part of **the sun** was smitten, and the third part of the moon, and the third part of the stars; so as the third part of them was darkened, and the day shone not for a third part of it, and the night likewise." (Revelation 8:12)*

*"And the fourth angel poured out his vial upon **the sun**; and power was given unto him to scorch men with fire. And men were scorched with great heat, and blasphemed the name of God, which hath power over these plagues: and they repented not to give him glory." (Revelation 16:8-9)*

In Revelation 8:12 we read that one third of the sun was darkened while in Revelation 16:8-9, we see that men were scorched with great heat. There seems to be a difference between the two passages, but if we look at them carefully, we will realize that they refer to the same thing.

If the sun is darkened by one third, it would have lost one third of its energy. The question is where does this energy go? An answer would be that this energy comes down to the earth. When one third of the sun's energy came upon the earth, men and women on the earth will be scorched.

	Revelation 8:12	Revelation 16:8-9
Common Denominator	"The sun"	"The sun"
Similar Event	The sun was smitten and the day shone not (The sun lost its solar energy to the Earth)	Men were scorched with great heat (The Earth gained solar heat from the sun)

THE FIFTH TRUMPET AND VIAL

*"And the fifth angel sounded, and I saw a star fall from heaven unto the earth: and to him was given the key of the bottomless pit. And he opened the bottomless pit; and there arose a smoke out of the pit, as the smoke of a great furnace; and the sun and the air were darkened by reason of the smoke of the pit. And there came out of the smoke locusts upon the earth: and unto them was given power, as the scorpions of the earth have power. And it was commanded them that they should not hurt the grass of the earth, neither any green thing, neither any tree; but only those men which have not the seal of God in their foreheads. And to them it was given that they should not kill them, but that they should be tormented five months: and **their torment was as the torment of a scorpion**, when he striketh a man. And in those days shall men seek death, and shall not find it; and shall desire to die, and death shall flee from them. And the shapes of the locusts were like unto horses prepared unto battle; and on their heads were as it were crowns like gold, and their faces were as the faces of men. And they had hair as the hair of women, and their teeth were as the teeth of lions. And they had breastplates, as it were breastplates of iron; and the sound of their wings was as the sound of chariots of many horses running to battle. And they had tails like unto scorpions,*

and there were stings in their tails: and their power was to hurt men five months. And they had a king over them, which is the angel of the bottomless pit, whose name in the Hebrew tongue is Abaddon, but in the Greek tongue hath his name Apollyon." (Revelation 9:1-11)

*"And the fifth angel poured out his vial upon the seat of the beast; and his kingdom was full of darkness; and they gnawed their tongues for pain, And blasphemed the God of heaven because of **their pains and their sores**, and repented not of their deeds." (Revelation 16:10-11)*

Revelation 16:10-11 talks about men cursing God because they are tormented by pains and sores, and in Revelation 9:1-11, we read of the locusts coming out of the bottomless pit. These locusts could be symbolic language of advanced military aircrafts that we have today or they could be literal supernatural creatures that will be released when the Fifth Trumpet is sounded. They will fly like locusts but sting like scorpions.

We know what happens when a person is stung by a scorpion. First you feel the pain and then a sore develops. This is what Revelation 16:10-11 is talking about – pain and sore. You may remember that when the Israelites were in the wilderness and they murmured against God, He released fiery serpents in the midst of their camp (Numbers 21:6). In the case here, these supernatural creatures (or advanced military aircrafts and weapons) are released and it could be that the poison injected in the sting render their victims incapable of thinking, leaving them in such a condition of pain that they would wish they could die but will be unable to kill themselves.

	Revelation 9:1-11	Revelation 16:10-11
Similar Event	Strange creatures were tormenting men	Men were tormented with pains and sores

THE SIXTH TRUMPET AND VIAL

*"And the sixth angel sounded, and I heard a voice from the four horns of the golden altar which is before God, saying to the sixth angel which had the trumpet, Loose the four angels which are bound in **the great river Euphrates**. And the four angels were loosed, which were prepared for an hour, and a day, and a month, and a year, for to slay the third part of men." (Revelation 9:13-15)*

*"And the sixth angel poured out his vial upon **the great river Euphrates**; and the water thereof was dried up, that the way of the kings of the east might be prepared. And I saw three unclean spirits like frogs come out of the mouth of the dragon, and out of the mouth of the beast, and out of the mouth of the false prophet. For they are the spirits of devils, working miracles, which go forth unto the kings of the earth and of the whole world, to gather them to the battle of that great day of God Almighty. Behold, I come as a thief. Blessed is he that watcheth, and keepeth his garments, lest he walk naked, and they see his shame. And he gathered them together into a place called in the Hebrew tongue Armageddon." (Revelation 16:12-16)*

The common denominator here is the River Euphrates. Revelation 9:14-15 talks about four angels that were loosed from the River Euphrates. These angels are supernatural beings which are restrained by God from operating. The moment the Sixth Trumpet is blown, God's restraint on these angels will be removed. The war at the River Euphrates revealed through the Sixth Trumpet and the Sixth Vial will be like no other war that has been fought in the history of mankind. It will be the most terrible and awesome war that the world will ever witness.

Revelation 9:16 tells us that some two hundred million soldiers will be involved:

"And the number of the army of the horsemen were two hundred thousand thousand: and I heard the number of them." (Revelation 9:16)

Why will there be so many men involved in that one war? Revelation 16:13-14 gives us the answer:

"And I saw three unclean spirits like frogs come out of the mouth of the dragon, and out of the mouth of the beast, and out of the mouth of the false prophet. For they are the spirits of devils, working miracles, which go forth unto the kings of the earth and of the whole world, to gather them to the battle of that great day of God Almighty." (Revelation 16:13-14)

Three unclean spirits are involved in deceiving the kings of the nations of the earth to battle. It is actually referring to Satan, the Antichrist, and the False Prophet, who are the deceivers of the nations, gathering them for this final showdown in the valley of Jehoshaphat. This is what the prophet Joel prophesied concerning the Day of the Lord:

"For, behold, in those days, and in that time, when I shall bring again the captivity of Judah and Jerusalem, I will also gather all nations, and will bring them down into the valley of Jehoshaphat, and will plead with them there for my people and for my heritage Israel, whom they have scattered among the nations, and parted my land." (Joel 3:1-2)

"Let the heathen be wakened, and come up to the valley of Jehoshaphat: for there will I sit to judge all the heathen round about. Put ye in the sickle, for the harvest is ripe: come, get you down; for the press is full, the fats overflow; for their wickedness is great. Multitudes, multitudes in the valley of decision: for the day of the LORD is near in the valley of decision." (Joel 3:12-14)

Immediately after the deception by the three unclean spirits, the four angels that have been restrained until that moment will be released and they will unleash the destructive forces in the nations and the worst and most disastrous war in human history will explode in the Middle East.

The River Euphrates is one of the most important rivers in the world because the history of mankind **began** at this river. Hence the history of the human race, as we know it, will also **end** here and a new history under the rule and reign of the King of kings and Lord of lords will begin. Isn't this exciting?

The Euphrates River is also important because it is the northern-most boundary of the land promised by God to Abraham. We read of this in Joshua chapter one:

"From the wilderness and this Lebanon even unto the great river, the river Euphrates, all the land of the Hittites, and unto the great sea toward the going down of the sun, shall be your coast." (Joshua 1:4)

We know that the boundary of Israel today is not the boundary described in Joshua chapter one. In fact, when Israel was re-gathered as a nation in 1948, she only occupied a small part of that which was described in the book of Joshua. But ever since 1948, Israel has moved south and east and has taken back the West Bank, the Golan Heights, the city of Jerusalem and other places. One day, the covenant-keeping God will fulfill His promise by giving to Israel all the land He has promised Abraham in covenant. The nations of the world will be enraged by this and thus they shall gather for war against Israel. This battle is called the Battle of Armageddon.

"And he gathered them together into a place called in the Hebrew tongue Armageddon." (Revelation 16:16)

	Revelation 9:13-21	Revelation 16:12-16
Common Denominator	"The great river Euphrates"	"The great river Euphrates"
Similar Event	A great and awesome war	The Battle of Armageddon

THE SEVENTH TRUMPET AND VIAL

"And the seventh angel sounded; and there were great voices in heaven, saying, The kingdoms of this world are become the kingdoms of our Lord, and of his Christ; and he shall reign for ever and ever. And the four and twenty elders, which sat before God on their seats, fell upon their faces, and worshipped God, saying, We give thee thanks, O LORD God Almighty, which art, and wast, and art to come; because thou hast taken to thee thy great power, and hast reigned. And the

*nations were angry, and thy wrath is come, and the time of the dead, that they should be judged, and that thou shouldest give reward unto thy servants the prophets, and to the saints, and them that fear thy name, small and great; and shouldest destroy them which destroy the earth. And the temple of God was opened in heaven, and there was seen in his temple the ark of his testament: **and there were lightnings, and voices, and thunderings, and an earthquake, and great hail.**" (Revelation 11:15-19)*

One of the reasons for the second coming of Christ is to save this earth from nuclear destruction. The nuclear holocaust which will take place in the Middle East will lead to total annihilation of mankind if God does not intervene. The prophet Ezekiel speaks of hailstones coming down from heaven which is one of God's means of destroying the armies of the world.

"And I will plead against him with pestilence and with blood; and I will rain upon him, and upon his bands, and upon the many people that are with him, an overflowing rain, and great hailstones, fire, and brimstone. Thus will I magnify myself, and sanctify myself; and I will be known in the eyes of many nations, and they shall know that I am the LORD." (Ezekiel 38:22-23)

The battle of Armageddon will destroy about one third of mankind. This third part of men seems to be mentioned repeatedly in all the trumpets. The First Trumpet talks about a third part of the trees. The Second Trumpet mentioned the third part of the sea. The Third Trumpet, the third part of the waters. The Fourth Trumpet, the third part of the moon, stars and sun. What exactly does this "one third" represent? Let's turn to Revelation chapter twelve for this.

*"And there appeared another wonder in heaven; and behold a great red dragon, having seven heads and ten horns, and seven crowns upon his heads. **And his tail drew the third part of the stars of heaven**, and did cast them to the earth: and the dragon stood before the woman which was ready to be delivered, for to devour her child as soon as it was born." (Revelation 12:3-4)*

We can deduce that the one third is **representative** of those who followed Satan. The dragon represents Satan and when "his tail drew the third part of the stars of heaven", one third of the angels followed him in his rebellion against God. It is common for the "head" to speak of leadership and the "tail" to speak of followers.

Let us now take a look at the Seventh Vial:

*"And the seventh angel poured out his vial into the air; and there came a great voice out of the temple of heaven, from the throne, saying, It is done. **And there were voices, and thunders, and lightnings; and there was a great earthquake**, such as was not since men were upon the earth, so mighty an earthquake, and so great. And the great city was divided into three parts, and the cities of the nations fell: and great Babylon came in remembrance before God, to give unto her the cup of the wine of the fierceness of his wrath. And every island fled away, and the mountains were not found. And there **fell upon men a great hail** out of heaven, every stone about the weight of a talent: and men blasphemed God because of the plague of the hail; for the plague thereof was exceeding great." (Revelation 16:17-21)*

The Seventh Vial tells us of a literal earthquake that will take place, the likes of which have never been seen before. Ezekiel 38:19-20 speaks of the same thing:

*"For in my jealousy and in the fire of my wrath have I spoken, Surely in that day there shall be a **great shaking** in the land of Israel; so that the fishes of the sea, and the fowls of the heaven, and the beasts of the field, and all creeping things that creep upon the earth, and all the men that are upon the face of the earth, shall shake at my presence, and the mountains shall be thrown down, and the steep places shall fall, and every wall shall fall to the ground." (Ezekiel 38:19-20)*

Look at the similar language used – mountains shall be thrown down, mountains not found, steep places will fall, and the great city will be divided into three parts.

Revelation 16:21 tells us that the hailstones that will fall down from heaven will each weigh a talent, which is equivalent to one hundred pounds. This plague of hail will be exceedingly great and will destroy the armies that will come against the nation of Israel. Thus the Sixth Vial is the Battle of Armageddon while the Seventh Vial is the end of that great war.

	Revelation 11:15-19	Revelation 16:17-21
Common Denominator	"There were lightnings, and voices, and thunderings, and an earthquake, and great hail"	"There were voices, and thunderings, and lightnings, and there was a great earthquake …and there fell upon men a great hail"
Similar Event	Plague of the hail	Plague of the hail

OTHER POSSIBILITIES

Another possibility for the first four judgments of God to happen can be fulfilled by a nuclear war. Regarding the Fourth Trumpet and Fourth Vial, the likeliness of this plague being the heat caused by a thermonuclear explosion is quite probable. The darkening of the sun, moon, and stars could be the result of the nuclear dust in the atmosphere reducing the visibility of the sun, moon, and stars. The men being scorched by heat could be the Fourth Vial's description of the effect of the heat due to radiation produced by a nuclear explosion. The Fourth Vial therefore emphasizes the effect of a nuclear war on men while the Fourth Trumpet emphasizes the effect on the atmosphere.

If this is so, then we can see the Third Trumpet and Vial as contamination of drinking water by nuclear fallout and/or the use of biological and chemical weapons. The Second Trumpet and Vial will then be the effect of nuclear and/or biological and chemical weapons on the oceans and seas. The First Trumpet and Vial will be their effect on land.

First Trumpet/Vial	Effect of a nuclear explosion upon the earth
Second Trumpet/Vial	Effect of a nuclear explosion upon the oceans
Third Trumpet/Vial	Contamination of drinking water by a nuclear fallout
Fourth Trumpet/Vial	Effect of a nuclear explosion on the earth's atmosphere

Modern science therefore has created military technology capable of fulfilling these plagues in the wrath of God. This does not mean that the wrath of God cannot be fulfilled by supernatural acts of God. It is very possible that they are all supernatural acts executed by angels.

So this is the sequence of events from the First Trumpet/Vial to the Seventh Trumpet/Vial. We have seen that the trumpets and the vials are actually parallel events and why God double-mentions it. In any event, all of us who are born again and have put our trust in the finished redemptive work of Jesus Christ unto the very end will no longer be around when these events take place. We would all have been caught up to meet the Lord in the air, rejoicing with Him while all these events take place on the earth. Is there a smile on your face yet?

Chapter 9

THE LAST TRUMPET

We have now seen in the preceding chapters the entire sequence of events leading to the Day of the Lord and the events that come after it. I believe that I have laid out for the reader these events in a way that is clear and easy to understand so that there is no room for any doubt or confusion. Be that as it may, I am very much aware that there will still be all sorts of questions lingering in the minds of readers, because the teaching that the Church will be raptured before the Great Tribulation is so embedded in our belief system. As such, what I have presented hitherto might come as a shock to the belief system of most Christians as far as eschatology is concerned. As I mentioned in the introduction section of this book, my purpose for writing this book is to dissolve any uncertainty regarding the understanding of the book of Revelation. In this chapter, therefore, we want to zoom in and take a closer look at this hotly-debated issue regarding the Rapture of the Church.

THE LAST TRUMPET

One of the main reasons why many Bible teachers and preachers teach about the Church escaping the Great Tribulation centres around their interpretation of the trumpet in First Thessalonians chapter four (please note that this trumpet has got nothing to do with the seven trumpets that we have looked at in the preceding chapter). So let us turn to that text again:

"For the Lord himself shall descend from heaven with a shout, with the voice of the archangel, and with the trump of God: and the dead in Christ shall rise first: then we which are alive and remain shall be caught up together with them

in the clouds, to meet the Lord in the air: and so shall we ever be with the Lord."
(1 Thessalonians 4:16-17)

We have already established three things in this passage:

1. The Lord Jesus shall descend from heaven.
2. The dead in Christ shall rise.
3. We that are alive will be caught up together with them in the clouds to meet the Lord in the air.

In order for those of us who still are alive to be caught up with them in the clouds, we must be changed. Changed to what? Our mortal physical body must be changed into a glorious, incorruptible body. No more arthritis, no more diabetes, no more bad cholesterol, oh glory! Paul mentioned this in his letter to the Corinthian church:

*"Behold, I shew you a mystery; we shall not all sleep, but we shall all be changed, in a moment, in the twinkling of an eye, at the last trump: for the trumpet shall sound, and the dead shall be raised incorruptible, and **we shall be changed**. For this corruptible must put on **incorruption**, and this mortal must put on **immortality**." (1 Corinthians 15:51-53)*

THE SAME TRUMPET?

In 1 Thessalonians 4:16-17, Paul said that when the trumpet of God is sounded, we will be raptured together with the dead in Christ. Next, we read in 1 Corinthians 15:52 that at the last trumpet, the dead shall be raised incorruptible and we shall be changed. This leads us to a very important question: is there just one resurrection of the dead in Christ and one occasion when we are transformed into the likeness of Christ or are there two different periods of time when this takes place? Are these two passages talking about different events or are they both referring to the same thing?

There are many that teach that the resurrection of the dead and the rapture of the Church in 1 Thessalonians 4:16-17 is different from that in First Corinthians chapter fifteen. They also say that the trumpet Jesus talked about in Matthew 24:31 is also different from the trumpet in First Thessalonians chapter four. Let us take a look at Matthew 24:31 again:

"And he shall send his angels with a great sound of a trumpet, and they shall gather together his elect from the four winds, from one end of heaven to the other." (Matthew 24:31)

It is pretty obvious that the trumpets mentioned in Matthew 24:31, 1 Corinthians 15:52 and 1 Thessalonians 4:16-17 are all referring to the same trumpet. Why? Because the same things happen.

1 Thessalonians 4:16-17 states that when the trumpet is sounded, the dead in Christ will rise and we that are alive and remain will be caught up to meet the Lord in the air. 1 Corinthians 15:51-53 says that when the trumpet is sounded, the dead in Christ will rise and we will be changed from having a corruptible physical body to one that is incorruptible. Matthew 24:31 states that when the trumpet is sounded, the angels will gather Christ's elect from the four winds, that is, from the four corners of the earth. It does not take a theologian to figure this out.

Here's a neat way of summing it up:

1 Thessalonians 4	1 Corinthians 15	Matthew 24
Trumpet	Trumpet	Trumpet
Resurrection	Resurrection	
Rapture	Transformation	Rapture

Since we all know by now that the resurrection of the dead in Christ precedes the Rapture from the passage in First Thessalonians chapter four, when the resurrection is being mentioned in First Corinthians chapter fifteen, we can safely conclude that what follows must be the Rapture. We can also conclude that the resurrection must take place in Matthew chapter twenty-four since the Rapture is mentioned there. Therefore the three passages are parallel and the **trumpets are one and the same**. They just describe the event from different angles.

However, those who teach that the Rapture will take place before the Great Tribulation contend that First Thessalonians chapter four speaks about a special resurrection and they call it the out-resurrection. In other words, they are talking about a resurrection other than the main resurrection of the dead in Christ. They say that the trumpet in First Thessalonians chapter four is different from the trumpet mentioned in Matthew chapter twenty-four.

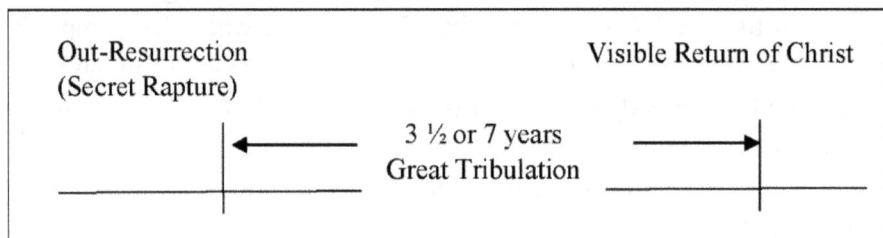

Out-Resurrection (Secret Rapture)   Visible Return of Christ

3 ½ or 7 years   Great Tribulation

Let us find out whether there is any truth to this type of teaching.

In his first letter to the Corinthians, chapter fifteen and verse fifty-two, Paul used the phrase *"the last trumpet"*. The entire chapter fifteen of First Corinthians is also known as the "Resurrection Chapter" and Paul said here that the resurrection of the dead in Christ will take place **only at the last trumpet**.

Therefore logic dictates that if the resurrection takes place only at the last trumpet, then it definitely cannot take place at a "second" last trumpet! Hence there is only one trumpet by which *all* the dead in Christ shall be raised. What Paul is saying so clearly is that there is only one resurrection of the dead in Christ and it will take place when the last trumpet is sounded.

If the trumpet mentioned in First Thessalonians chapter four is a different trumpet, then it has to be referring to a "second" last trumpet. If there is a second last trumpet in the resurrection of the dead in Christ, then Paul must have taught it in First Corinthians chapter fifteen. However, if we read that chapter carefully, we will notice that when Paul talked about the resurrection of the dead in Christ, he did not mention two separate resurrections. He mentioned **only one** resurrection of the dead in Christ and that takes place **only** at the sound of the last trumpet.

At the risk of repeating myself too often, the last trumpet in First Corinthians chapter fifteen *is* the same trumpet mentioned First Thessalonians chapter four and Matthew chapter twenty-four.

THE SHOUT, THE VOICE AND THE TRUMPET

Now let us take a look at the counter-argument given by those who say that the trumpet in 1 Thessalonians 4:16-17 is different from the one in Matthew 24:31. We need to cover all bases so as to leave no room for any doubt. Here is the argument:

In Matthew 24:31, Jesus only said that He shall send His angels when the trumpet is sounded. The verse does not say that the Lord shall descend from heaven with a shout and with the voice of an archangel. So they conclude that since First Thessalonians chapter four has a shout, a voice of an archangel and a trumpet call, it must be talking about a different event. They contend that there are three things in 1 Thessalonians 4:16-17 whereas there is only one in Matthew 24:31.

1 Thessalonians 4:16	Matthew 24:31
1. Shout 2. Voice 3. Trumpet	1. Trumpet

What is the explanation to this proposition? Well, let us first look at where Paul got his shout and where he got his voice of the archangel when he wrote to the church at Thessalonica.

I want you to notice that in 1 Thessalonians 4:15, Paul mentioned how he came to the understanding about what will happen on the day of the resurrection of the dead in Christ.

*"For this we say to you **by the word of the Lord**, that we which are alive and remain unto the coming of the Lord shall not prevent them which are asleep." (1 Thessalonians 4:15)*

So how did Paul get his understanding? He received his understanding from the Scriptures alone, by the word of the Lord! There was no hint of extra-biblical revelation given to him; he understood these things from the Scriptures. Since that is the case, let us go back then to the Scriptures and let us see whether on the Day of the Lord, when He returns and His trumpet is blown, will there be a voice? Will there be a shout?

First of all, we need to understand the background behind Matthew 24:31. If we look at verse twenty-nine of the same chapter, we realize that the heavenly Blackout takes place. The sun and the moon shall be darkened, and the stars shall not give off their light. Now we have already established in chapter six of this book that Matthew 24:31 is the Day of the Lord.

Let us turn to a parallel passage that speaks of the Day of the Lord in the Old Testament:

The sun and the moon shall be darkened, and the stars shall withdraw their shining. The LORD also shall roar out of Zion, and utter his voice from Jerusalem; and the heavens and the earth shall shake: but the LORD will be the hope of His people, and the strength of the children of Israel." (Joel 3:15-16)

Therefore, we will notice that immediately after the Blackout, there will be two other things that will occur:

1. There will be a roar

2. There will be a voice

What is a roar? A roar is the shout of a lion. When a lion is angry, it roars. When Jesus returns, He will come as the Lion of the tribe of Judah. Why will He come as the Lion of Judah? Because at the time of the coming of Christ, the very existence of the nation of Israel will be threatened. Israel will be under the attack of the armies of the world and the natural seed of Abraham will be at the brink of being annihilated. Apart from establishing His millennial rule on the earth, the Lord will return for two basic reasons:

---

1. To prevent the nation of Israel from total annihilation

2. To prevent the Church from being wiped out

The Antichrist will go on a rampage to kill Christians and Jews. If God does not intervene, the whole nation of Israel will be totally wiped out. Satan has attempted to destroy God's covenant people, the Jews, at different periods of human history. The last was during the Holocaust, when Adolf Hitler exterminated six million Jews during the Second World War. The next attempt of such scale will take place when the Antichrist sets up his image in the Jewish temple in Jerusalem. After three and a half years of Great Tribulation, Israel will be invaded by many nations. Joel chapter three describes this scenario. Jesus will then come back as the Lion of Judah. He will be angry at the nations that seek to destroy Israel, and in His anger, He shall come upon the nations with a roar.

Here's another passage from the prophet Isaiah:

*"The LORD shall go forth as a mighty man, he shall stir up jealousy like a man of war: **he shall cry, yea, roar**, he shall prevail against his enemies. I have long time holden my peace; I have been still, and refrained myself: **now will I cry like a travailing woman**; I shall destroy and devour at once." (Isaiah 42:13-14)*

Again, we see that when the Lord comes to fight for Israel in that Day, He will roar. He will no longer hold back, but He will pour out His wrath through the seven trumpets/vials upon the nations that come against Israel.

So you will notice that Paul did not get any extra-biblical revelation and he did not invent some strange doctrines. When he wrote to the Thessalonians in his first epistle, chapter four, he was not talking about a separate resurrection. When Jesus comes on the Day of the Lord, there will be a trumpet according to Matthew chapter twenty-four. According to Joel, there will be a shout and there will be a voice uttered from Zion. So what do we have here? We have an eschatological equation:

1 Thessalonians 4:16   =   Matthew 24:31   +   Joel 3:16

The reason we can combine these verses from Matthew and Joel together and equate them to the one in First Thessalonians is because they all talk about the same occasion – the Day of the Lord!

Joel 3:16 mentions a shout and a voice **after the Blackout**. Matthew 24:31 mentions a trumpet **after the Blackout**. We have seen from Joel 2:31 that the Blackout comes **before** the Day of the Lord. Thus Joel 3:16 and Matthew 24:31 are both dealing with the Day of the Lord.

In 1 Thessalonians 4:16, three things are mentioned – trumpet, shout and voice, and **they all take place** on the Day of the Lord. In Matthew 24:31, on the Day of the Lord, there will be a trumpet. In Joel 3:16, on the Day of the Lord, there will be a shout and a voice. Hence we can see that they all have a common denominator – THE DAY OF THE LORD!

```
<---------------------------- DAY OF THE LORD ---------------------------->


    1 Thessalonians 4:16    =    Matthew 24:31    +    Joel 3:16
    Trumpet                      Trumpet               Shout
    Shout                                              Voice
    Voice
```

The apostle Paul therefore did not teach about two resurrections or a trumpet before the last trumpet. Paul specifically said that only at the last trumpet will the dead in Christ rise from the dead. It simply means that there will **never** be another trumpet before that last trumpet when the dead in Christ shall rise.

Chapter 10

THE RAPTURE - MISTAKEN NOTIONS

At this stage, I believe that things are beginning to come together for the reader. Yet I still suspect that there are many reading this book that are still numb from the shock to their belief system. I fully understand and I do not fault the reader because that was what happened to me too. You see, I, like many believers, was brought up with the belief that we are going to be raptured before the Great Tribulation, thinking that the Great Tribulation includes the pouring out of the wrath of God. But when the Lord opened my eyes through my study of the Scriptures, it took me a bit of time to realign and renew my mind to the truth of His Word. It is just like when God began to restore the truth that it is His will to heal and prosper His people. If we are brought up with the belief that God does not want His people healed and prosperous, then we will find it difficult initially to accept the truth that nothing pleases our heavenly Father more than to see His children healed, prosperous and whole.

Back to the subject at hand – the Rapture of the Church. We will continue to examine in-depth the many issues and burning questions surrounding this topic. We want to resolve as many, if not all, questions that are still on the mind of the reader.

Let us look at the three main views held by Christians concerning the timing of the Rapture. Many hold the view that Jesus will return secretly before the Great Tribulation to take them in a secret Rapture. This is called the **pre-tribulation** view.

PRE-TRIBULATION RAPTURE

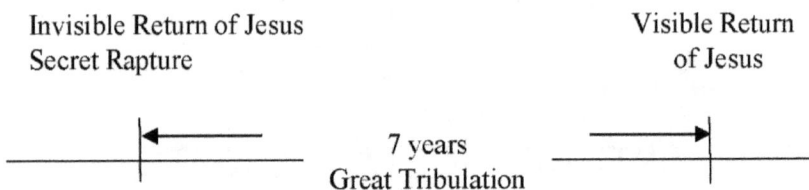

Invisible Return of Jesus
Secret Rapture

Visible Return
of Jesus

7 years
Great Tribulation

Another variation is the view held by the **mid-tribulationists** which differ from the pre-tribulationists only in the length of the Great Tribulation. Instead of seven years, they believe that it is only three and a half years.

MID-TRIBULATION RAPTURE

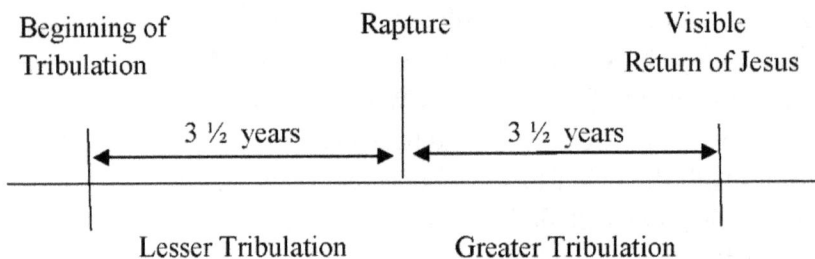

Beginning of
Tribulation

Rapture

Visible
Return of Jesus

3 ½ years

3 ½ years

Lesser Tribulation

Greater Tribulation

Both believe that the Church will escape the Great Tribulation in a secret Rapture at a secret and invisible coming of Jesus Christ. In this sense, the mid-tribulationists are, in essence, pre-tribulation in doctrine with the exception that the Great Tribulation (from which they believe they will escape) is only three and a half years in length. So in this chapter, we shall treat them both as pre-tribulationists.

Finally there is the **post-tribulation** view.

POST-TRIBULATION RAPTURE

| Beginning of | | Visible Return of Jesus |
| Great Tribulation | | Rapture |

Great Tribulation

7 Years

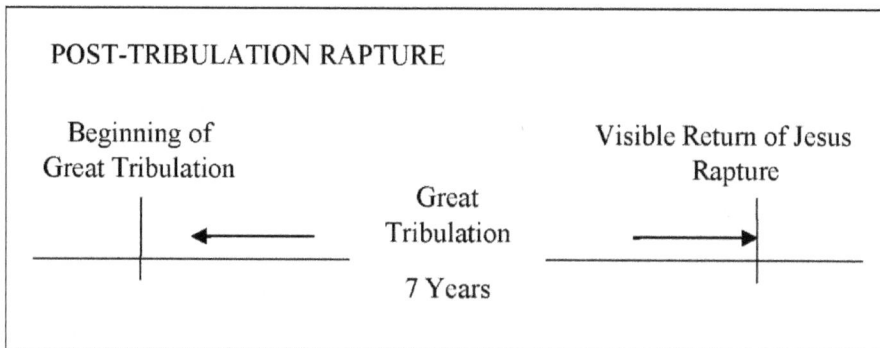

However, this is a traditional post-tribulation view in the sense that the Great Tribulation also includes the wrath of God. This is also erroneous because by the time the Great Tribulation (Fifth Seal) is over, the Blackout (Sixth Seal) takes place, Jesus returns on the Day of the Lord and the Church is raptured.

There are several reasons why these views are erroneous in the study of Eschatology. They will be treated under the following three sections:

1. Mistaken notions
2. Mistaken identities
3. Misquotations

We will deal with the mistaken notions in this chapter.

FIRST MISTAKEN NOTION

The pre-tribulation Rapture was the teaching held by the Church right from the beginning

---

You see, most Christians do not realize that the pre-tribulation doctrine was never taught nor held by the early Church in the book of Acts until the year 1830. Unfortunately, we have assumed that this has been the Church's teaching right from the beginning, which is a grievous mistake.

Dr. Martin Lloyd-Jones, in his book, "Prove All Things", relates how the Church came to hold the pre-tribulation view that the Church will not have to go through the Tribulation before the Rapture. Here's an excerpt from his book:

> *"There has been a teaching which has gained great popularity in evangelical circles, concerning what is known as 'the secret Rapture of the saints'. It teaches that the Lord at His second coming will appear only to His saints, and that they will be raptured into the heavens secretly with nobody seeing it, nobody knowing anything at all about it; all they know is that suddenly the saints will have gone.*
>
> *I wonder whether you know the history and the story of that teaching? The people who hold it seem to assume that this has been the teaching of the Church, that it is truly biblical teaching, but do you know its history? The answer is that this teaching was first put forward in 1830. It had never been heard of before.*
>
> *How then did it start? The answer is most interesting; again we must bring in the name of Edward Irving. In about 1830 the people who had become known as the Plymouth Brethren, including such names as J.N. Darby, B.W. Newton and S.P. Tregelles, and others of the early first leaders of the Brethren movement, began to gather together with Edward Irving and some of his followers to hold what they called Prophetic Conferences. They became interested in the whole doctrine of our Lord's second coming, and they said, 'This has been neglected and we must look into it and we must examine it.' So they held conferences at a place called Powerscourt. And it was in connection with those conferences that this whole idea of the secret Rapture of the saints came in. We have the authority of S.P. Tregelles, a great and famous biblical scholar, who tells us how it happened in a book he wrote called 'The Hope of Christ's Second Coming'. In it he says, 'I am not aware that there was any definite teaching that there should be a secret Rapture of the Church at a secret Coming until this was*

given forth as an "utterance" [notice his inverted commas] in Mr. Irving's church from what was then received as being the voice of the Spirit. But whether anyone asserted such a thing or not, it was from that supposed revelation that the modern doctrine and the modern phraseology respecting it arose.' Tregelles attended these conferences, so he speaks with authority.

In Edward Irving's church they claimed that the gifts of the Spirit had all been restored, prophetic utterances among them, and it was through one of these supposed utterances of the Spirit that this idea of the secret Rapture of the saints came in. So this was something that they claimed the Spirit had given as a direct revelation, and they accepted it. What is amazing is that a man like J.N. Darby accepted it, but he did, and continued to teach it, and it had been taught very commonly ever since then. Tregelles would not accept it, neither would B.W. Newton. It was the first cause of a division amongst the Plymouth Brethren. (Incidentally, J.N. Darby very soon saw the dangerous tendencies in Edward Irving and entirely broke with him, but he continued to accept the secret Rapture solely as the result of what claimed to be a prophetic utterance.)"

So, you see, the pre-tribulation teaching did not exist in the early Church and only became popular in 1830 due to a "prophetic utterance". Please understand that I am not against prophetic utterances. I am all for the five-fold offices of the apostles, prophets, evangelists, pastors and teachers. I am all for the operation of the nine gifts of the Holy Spirit in the Church. However, God's Word also says to test every prophecy (see 1 Thessalonians 5:20-21). To test a prophecy simply means to find out whether the prophetic word lines up with the whole counsel of the Word of God. In other words, prophetic utterances do not validate Scriptures; Scriptures validate prophetic utterances.

SECOND MISTAKEN NOTION

God will not allow those who love Him to go through
the Great Tribulation

The second mistaken notion of the pre-tribulation teaching is that God will not allow those who love Him to go through the Great Tribulation. However, this would run against the grain of Scriptures throughout the Bible.

Jesus obviously advocated enduring tribulation rather than escaping it. He even assured us that we will have victory over it:

> *"These things I have spoken unto you, that in Me ye might have peace.* **In the world ye shall have tribulation***: but be of good cheer; I have overcome the world." (John 16:33)*

This verse does not just apply to our everyday tribulations of life; it applies to **all** tribulations, including the Great Tribulation. So be of good cheer, Jesus will give us the grace to overcome the Great Tribulation.

Paul and Barnabas exhorted the saints in Asia Minor to enter into the kingdom of God through much tribulation:

> *"Confirming the souls of the disciples, and exhorting them to continue in the faith, and that* **we must through much tribulation** *enter into the kingdom of God." (Acts 14:22)*

Paul himself gloried in tribulation:

> *"And not only so,* **but we glory in tribulation also: knowing that tribulation worketh patience***; and patience, experience; and experience, hope." (Romans 5:3-4)*

The word "glory" in Romans 5:3 is *kauchaomai* in Greek and can also be translated as "joy" or "rejoice". Paul therefore rejoiced in tribulation knowing that it brings forth the fruit of patience. Now, this does not mean that Paul took pleasure in tribulation. It simply means that when he had to go through tribulation, he rejoiced because the grace of God is more than enough for Paul to **overcome** any tribulation.

If there was ever one worthy to escape tribulation, it would be John, who wrote of himself as the disciple whom Jesus loved (John 21:20). Yet in Revelation 1:9, John was presented as one who suffered for the Word of God:

*"I John, who also am your brother, and **companion in tribulation** and in the kingdom and patience of Jesus Christ was in the isle that is called Patmos for the word of God and for the testimony of Jesus Christ." (Revelation 1:9)*

The church of Smyrna was highly commended by the Lord Jesus, yet He never promised that she would not go through tribulation:

*"Fear none of those things **which thou shall suffer**: behold the devil shall cast some of you into prison, that ye may be tried; and **ye shall have tribulation** ten days: be thou faithful until death, and I will give thee the crown of life." (Revelation 2:10)*

Now, don't get me wrong. I am not advocating that Christians should go out and look for tribulation. Neither did Jesus nor any of the apostles. What the Scriptures are exhorting us to do is to rejoice when tribulation comes, because God will provide us the wherewithal to overcome any tribulation.

For the saints, tribulation comes in the form of persecution and other kinds of unjust attacks because of the Word of God and the testimony of Jesus Christ. Such has been the lot of the Church from the book of Acts until today. In fact, persecution has intensified today – just take a look at the vicious and relentless attacks of the liberal-left against wholesome and godly values. This is going to climax during the period of the Fifth Seal when Satan will unleash his fury on the Body of Christ through the Antichrist because believers will refuse to bow to his image or take his mark. It is therefore foolish to presume that since God loves us, we shall escape the Great Tribulation. In fact, those that the Lord loves dearly will be the prime candidates for such attacks!

This mistaken notion all boils down to the fact that we have confused the Great Tribulation (the Fifth Seal) with the wrath of God (the Seventh Seal).

Know for sure that our heavenly Father will not allow us to taste of His wrath because His wrath is reserved only for the wicked and everyone who has rejected the gospel of Jesus. However, God's Word never promised that His beloved children will escape tribulation, small or great. He has, however, promised that we will be victorious in the midst of tribulations.

THIRD MISTAKEN NOTION

> The Second Coming of Jesus will be invisible and secret

The third mistaken notion of many Christians is the belief in a secret and invisible second coming of Christ. There are several reasons for this mistaken notion.

1. First Reason

The first reason most Christians believe that the Church will disappear at the time of the Rapture is their failure to grasp the meaning of the words "caught up" as used in 1 Thessalonians 4:17:

*"Then we which are alive and remain shall be **caught up** together with them in the clouds to meet the Lord in the air: and so shall we ever be with the Lord." (1 Thessalonians 4:17)*

The words "caught up" have been changed to "raptured" and popularized by evangelists the world over. The original Greek word used for "caught" is the word *harpazō*, which means "to seize, pluck, snatch away, carry off by force" (Thayer). This is the same word used by Jesus in John chapter ten:

*"And I give unto them eternal life; and they shall never perish, neither shall any man **pluck** them out of my hand. My Father, which gave them me, is greater than all; and no man is able to **pluck** them out of my Father's hand." (John 10:28-29)*

In this passage, Jesus used the word *harpazō* for "pluck" and it is clear from the sense of the passage that it does not mean to make invisible or to disappear. Have a look at another two passages in John chapter ten and Matthew chapter thirteen:

*"But he that is an hireling, and not the shepherd, whose own the sheep are not, seeth the wolf coming, and leaveth the sheep, and fleeth: and the wolf **catcheth** them, and scattereth the sheep." (John 10:12)*

*"When any one heareth the word of the kingdom, and understandeth it not, then cometh the wicked one, and **catcheth** away that which was sown in his heart. This is he which received seed by the way side." (Matthew 13:19)*

Again, *harpazō* is used but this time, it means "catch". Certainly, it does not give us the idea of disappearing into thin air. Let us look at yet another two passages:

*"And from the days of John the Baptist until now the kingdom of heaven suffereth violence, and the violent **take** it by force." (Matthew 11:12)*

*"When Jesus therefore perceived that they would come and **take** him by force, to make him a king, he departed again into a mountain himself alone." (John 6:15)*

The Greek word for "take" in the above passages is – you guessed it – *harpazō*, and has the meaning of seizing and not vanishing.

It is therefore abundantly clear that the phrase "caught up" used in 1 Thessalonians 4:17 means "seized" or "carried away by force". In other words, when the Rapture happens, we do not disappear or vanish into thin air but we shall be seized or carried away or caught up.

2. Second Reason

The second reason for many Christians believing in the Body of Christ will do a disappearing act at the time of the Rapture is because of the misunderstanding of what Jesus said in Matthew 24:40-41:

*"Then shall two be in the field; the one shall be **taken**, and the other left. Two women shall be grinding at the mill; the one shall be **taken**, and the other left." (Matthew 24:40-41)*

Many believers interpret the word "taken" to mean "disappear". The Greek word used here for the word "taken" is the word *paralambano* which means "to receive near, to take to, to join to one's self" (Thayer). There is no suggestion of a disappearing act. Therefore it is presumptuous to conclude that in Matthew 24:40-41 Jesus was talking about a secret Rapture that would involve the disappearance of the Church. Quite a number of movies have been made on end-times depicting Christians just disappearing with no one knowing what happened. It is simply not biblical.

No conceivable reasons can be suggested for the need of such a secrecy. When Jesus was taken up into heaven, His disciples *saw* Him being taken up. Why then should the Church be taken up secretly? There is no reason or need to do so. The whole concept of a secret Rapture is based on a misconception of the seventeenth chapter of the gospel of Luke. So let us examine this theory and see if there is any truth to it.

3. Third Reason

There is a misconception among many Christians that Jesus taught a secret Rapture at a secret coming. This widespread belief in the Church is derived from a passage in Luke 17:34-37:

*"I tell you, in that night there shall be two men in one bed; the one shall be **taken**, and the other shall be left. Two women shall be grinding together; the one shall be **taken**, and the other left. Two men shall be in the field; the one shall be **taken**, and the other left. And they answered and said unto him, Where, Lord? And he said unto them, Wheresoever the body is, thither will the eagles be gathered together." (Luke 17:34-37)*

This passage describes the Rapture as the separation of the born-again believer from the unbeliever. The righteous are taken away while the unrighteous are left behind.

We have seen how it is erroneous to translate the word "taken" to mean "disappear". Let us now see if the Rapture takes place at a secret coming of the Lord. A brief glance at Luke chapter seventeen will throw much light on this passage. The kingdom of heaven is the main theme. Jesus' first coming is spiritual in that He came to establish the kingdom of God in the realm of the human heart.

"And when he was demanded of the Pharisees, when the kingdom of God should come, he answered them and said, The kingdom of God cometh not with observation: Neither shall they say, Lo here! or, lo there! for, behold, the kingdom of God is within you." (Luke 17:20-21)

The second coming is the Day of the Son of man. In using this expression, Jesus was referring to the book of Daniel chapter seven in which the Son of man was presented with the dominion, the glory, and the kingdom that all people, nations and languages should serve Him. This second coming of Jesus to receive the kingdom from the Ancient of Days is referred to as the Day of the Son of man.

"I beheld till the thrones were cast down, and the Ancient of days did sit, whose garment was white as snow, and the hair of his head like the pure wool: his throne was like the fiery flame, and his wheels as burning fire [...] I saw in the night visions, and, behold, one like the Son of man came with the clouds of heaven, and came to the Ancient of days, and they brought him near before him. And there was given him dominion, and glory, and a kingdom, that all people, nations, and languages, should serve him: his dominion is an everlasting dominion, which shall not pass away, and his kingdom that which shall not be destroyed." (Daniel 7:9, 13, 14)

In Luke chapter seventeen, Jesus was speaking concerning His second coming to establish His kingdom and He said that the Day of the Son of man will come like lightning shining from the east to the west.

"For as the lightning, that lighteneth out of the one part under heaven, shineth unto the other part under heaven; so shall also the Son of man be in his day." (Luke 17:24)

This means that the second coming of Christ will be with light and sound since lightning is a flash of light followed by the sound of thunder. Many passages in the Bible agree with a visible appearance of Christ when He comes to establish His kingdom.

*"And then shall **appear** the sign of the Son of man in heaven." (Matthew 24:30)*

*"Behold, he cometh with clouds; and **every eye shall see him**, and they also which pierced him: and all kindreds of the earth shall wail because of him. Even so, Amen." (Revelation 1:7)*

Therefore Jesus cannot contradict Himself in the latter half of the seventeenth chapter of Luke by teaching a secret Rapture where Christians are raptured suddenly. You see, "one shall be taken, the other left" takes place on the Day when the Son of man is **revealed**, which is the Day of the Lord!

*"Even thus shall it be in **the day when the Son of man is revealed**. In that day, he which shall be upon the housetop, and his stuff in the house, let him not come down to take it away: and he that is in the field, let him likewise not return back." (Luke 17:30-31)*

The word "revealed" used in verse 30 is the Greek word *apokaluptō*, which means "to uncover, to make known, make manifest, lay open what has been veiled or covered up". As you can see, there is absolutely no way that it can be taken to imply a secret and invisible coming. The following passage of Scriptures prove it.

*"Let no man deceive you by any means: for that day shall not come, except there come a falling away first, and that man of sin be **revealed**, the son of perdition; who opposeth and exalteth himself above all that is called God, or that is worshipped; so that he as God sitteth in the temple of God, shewing himself that he is God. Remember ye not, that, when I was yet with you, I told you these things? And now ye know what withholdeth that he might be **revealed** in his time. For the mystery of iniquity doth already work: only he who now letteth will let, until he be taken out of the way. And then shall that Wicked be **revealed**, whom the Lord shall consume with the spirit of his mouth, and shall destroy with the brightness of his coming:" (2 Thessalonians 2:3-8)*

In all three instances where the word "revealed" is used in the above passage, it is the Greek word *apokaluptō*. In other words, the manifestation of the Antichrist is the day of his *apokaluptō*. There is nothing invisible or secret about it.

Here are two more passages:

*"But rejoice, inasmuch as ye are partakers of Christ's sufferings; that, when his glory shall be **revealed**, ye may be glad also with exceeding joy." (1 Peter 4:13)*

*"The elders which are among you I exhort, who am also an elder, and a witness of the sufferings of Christ, and also a partaker of the glory that shall be **revealed**:" (1 Peter 5:1)*

The word *apokaluptō* is again used in 1 Peter 5:1 for the word "revealed" and in 1 Peter 4:13 the word used is *apokalupsis*. This word is derived from *apokaluptō* and carries the meaning of "laying bare, manifestation, appearance". Get the drift?

The day of the Son of man – the Day of the Lord – is therefore the day of His manifestation in power and glory. No secret coming! No secret Rapture! "One shall be taken, the other left" takes place on the Day of the revelation of Jesus Christ in the clouds, right after the Blackout. Did Jesus teach a secret coming followed by a secret Rapture? The answer is a definite *no*.

Now, some Bible teachers believe that we should not be taken, but left behind. They argue that to be taken means to be eaten by vultures! They base their claim upon the last verse of Luke chapter seventeen:

*"I tell you, in that night there shall be two men in one bed; the one shall be taken, and the other shall be left. Two women shall be grinding together; the one shall be taken, and the other left. Two men shall be in the field; the one shall be taken, and the other left. **And they answered and said unto him, Where, Lord? And he said unto them, Wheresoever the body is, thither will the eagles be gathered together.**" (Luke 17:34-37)*

This verse may seem difficult to understand but there are a few key words that will help us.

First, let us look at the question asked by Jesus' disciples. What did they mean by "Where, Lord?" While the disciples were not highly educated, they certainly were not dense. They certainly could not be asking, "Left where, Lord?" because that would be asking the obvious! Two men are asleep in bed, one is taken and the other left. Left where? In bed, of course! Two men are working in the field, one is taken, the other left. Left where? In the field, of course! Hence the question asked by the disciples can only mean *"Taken where, Lord?"*

Some bible teachers postulate that Luke 17:37 means that "to be taken" is to be eaten by eagles or vultures. Let us look at the illustrations Jesus gave for a deeper understanding. Drawing on the judgment of God by water and fire in the days of Noah and Lot, Jesus drove home an important truth: **before God destroys the wicked, He takes the righteous to a place of safety**. In other words, the righteous escapes the wrath of God! This agrees with the following Scripture:

"For God hath not appointed us to wrath, but to obtain salvation by our Lord Jesus Christ." (1 Thessalonians 5:9)

The pre-tribulationists got it wrong when they say that Noah escaped the tribulation. The flood was **not** the tribulation. The flood was the wrath of God in judgment upon the wicked in Noah's day. To conclude that the flood was symbolic of the Great Tribulation is simply ignoring the obvious. Likewise, Lot did not escape the tribulation; he escaped the wrath of God. The raining down of fire and brimstone was His wrath upon the cities of Sodom and Gomorrah.

There is an unmistakable, distinct difference between the Great Tribulation and the wrath of God. The former is the period when Christians suffer the wrath of the Antichrist (the Fifth Seal) while the latter is a totally different period when the wicked and everyone who has rejected the offer of salvation in Christ Jesus suffer the wrath of God (the Seventh Seal).

In the days of Noah, he and his family were **taken** to a place of safety (inside the ark) before the flood came. Likewise, in the case of Lot, he and his family were **taken** to a place of safety before God rained fire and brimstone upon Sodom and Gomorrah. In both cases, those who were **taken** escaped the wrath of God.

We have seen that the Day of the Lord is a day of vengeance, a day of God's wrath. Before God pours out His wrath, born-again believers will be taken to a place of safety, that is, with the Lord in the air. Therefore one shall be **taken** while the other is left. To be "taken" therefore is to **escape** the wrath of God. It is those who are left behind that will suffer the wrath of God.

Nonetheless, since some teach that to be taken is to be eaten by vultures, we must examine the verse carefully to cover all angles.

*"And they answered and said unto him, Where, Lord? And he said unto them, Wheresoever **the body is**, thither will the eagles be gathered together." (Luke 17:37)*

We have already determined that the question asked by the disciples means "Taken where, Lord?" So Jesus was going to tell them where. The key to understanding this verse lies in the word "body". Jesus did not use a plural noun, He used the singular. This was because He was drawing upon an illustration that the disciples understood so well. In the wilderness of Judea, when an animal dies, that body (or carcass) will be the centre of attraction of the gathering of birds of prey.

Likewise, in the Day of the Son of man, when Christ returns in power and glory, His "eagles" that are scattered in the wilderness of this world will hear the trumpet sound and be gathered together unto Him in the air! The Day of the Lord is a day of gathering!

*"And he shall send his angels with a great sound of a trumpet, and **they shall gather together his elect** from the four winds, from one end of the heaven to the other." (Matthew 24:31)*

*"Now we beseech you, brethren, by the coming of our Lord Jesus Christ, and by the **gathering together** unto him." (2 Thessalonians 2:1)*

In other words, the Lord Jesus Christ will be the centre of attraction and gather all His saints toward Him in the Day of the Son of man. Jesus therefore likened Himself to a powerful source of attraction and His saints are likened to eagles that are drawn to such a powerful source of attraction. Those that "are taken" are taken for a great gathering in the air. Jesus never suggested that those taken will be eaten by vultures and neither did He teach a secret coming followed by a secret Rapture.

Chapter 11

THE RAPTURE - MISTAKEN IDENTITIES

In this chapter, we will look at three mistaken identities that Christians make which contribute to the confusion of the timing of the Rapture of the Church. I would like to state that this is not an exercise to put down anyone's doctrinal position. This book is merely to straighten out any confusion that exists in the Body of Christ. In order to do so, we need to examine mistaken notions, mistaken identities, and misquotations so that believers have a sure footing in their understanding of eschatology.

FIRST MISTAKEN IDENTITY

> The Day of the Lord is actually the Great Tribulation

A pre-tribulation belief comes about as a result of identifying the Day of the Lord as the Great Tribulation. This is a fundamental error.

There are respectable Bible commentaries that state that the Day of the Lord is the Great Tribulation. However, I would like to respectfully point out that this error is not only putting the cart in front of the horse, it is mistaking the cart for the horse!

Let us take a look at two key verses again to reiterate our point:

*"Immediately **after** the tribulation of those days shall the sun be darkened, and the moon shall not give her light, and the stars shall fall from heaven, and the powers of the heavens shall be shaken." (Matthew 24:29)*

From this verse we know that the Blackout **comes after** the Great Tribulation.

```
Great Tribulation      →      Blackout
```

*"The sun shall be turned into darkness, and the moon into blood, **before** the great and terrible day of the LORD come." (Joel 2:31)*

From this verse, we know that the Blackout **comes before** the Day of the Lord.

```
Blackout      →      The Day of the Lord
```

Combining the two verses together we will have this sequence:

```
Great Tribulation   →   Blackout   →   The Day of the Lord
```

The conclusion is then obvious: the Day of the Lord **cannot** come until we see a cosmic Blackout which only takes place after the Great Tribulation has ended. Therefore, the Great Tribulation must come before the Day of the Lord!

You see, by identifying the Day of the Lord as the Great Tribulation, it has caused Christians to mistakenly conclude that Revelation chapter five until chapter eighteen is the Great Tribulation and the Church is secretly raptured in chapter four and will come back with Christ in chapter nineteen where a second Rapture takes place.

Revelation chapter 4	First Rapture
Revelation chapters 5-18	Great Tribulation
Revelation chapter 19	Second Rapture

We shall bring up the following two verses again that will put this interpretation to bed once and for all.

*"And I beheld when he had opened the sixth seal, and, lo, there was a great earthquake; **and the sun became black as sackcloth of hair, and the moon became as blood.**" (Revelation 6:12)*

It does not require a genius to read the above verse to know that the Sixth Seal is the Blackout. Reading Matthew 24:29 clearly tells us that when this Blackout takes place **the Great Tribulation is already over**.

*"Immediately **after the tribulation of those days** shall the sun be darkened, and the moon shall not give her light, and the stars shall fall from heaven, and the powers of the heavens shall be shaken." (Matthew 24:29)*

Therefore the Great Tribulation is over in Revelation 6:12. How, then, can Revelation chapters five to eighteen be the Great Tribulation when in chapter six, at the Sixth Seal, the Great Tribulation is already over? The Seventh Seal is therefore not talking about the Great Tribulation but it is the wrath of God in the Day of the Lord. The correct Scriptural interpretation is thus:

Revelation chapter 6:9-11	The Great Tribulation
Revelation chapter 7	The Rapture
Revelation chapters 8, 9, 11	The Wrath of God

The time sequence ends in Revelation chapter eleven when at the last trumpet of the Seventh Seal, Christ takes the kingdoms and the dead are raised and reward is given to His saints.

"And the seventh angel sounded; and there were great voices in heaven, saying, The kingdoms of this world are become the kingdoms of our Lord, and of his Christ; and he shall reign for ever and ever. [...] And the nations were angry, and thy wrath is come, and the time of the dead, that they should be judged, and that thou shouldest give reward unto thy servants the prophets, and to the saints, and them that fear thy name, small and great; and shouldest destroy them which destroy the earth. And the temple of God was opened in heaven, and there was seen in his temple the ark of his testament: and there were lightnings, and voices, and thunderings, and an earthquake, and great hail." (Revelation 11:15, 18-19)

The Great Tribulation is portrayed again in Revelation chapters twelve and thirteen but this time in detail. Chapter twelve describes the persecution of the Church by Satan through the Antichrist while chapter thirteen delves into the details of the Antichrist person. Failure to see this has caused a lot of difficulties and confusion for many students of eschatology, let alone the man on the street. No wonder so many Christians prefer to steer clear of this subject when, in fact, it is so simple to understand.

SECOND MISTAKEN IDENTITY

The second error made by many Bible teachers and students alike is mistaking the wrath of God for the Great Tribulation.

The Wrath of God is the Great Tribulation

In interpreting Seventh Seal, all pre-tribulationists call it the Great Tribulation. It is no wonder that countless number of Christians do not believe that God will allow the Church to go through the Great Tribulation if this is really so. If the Seventh Seal is indeed the Great Tribulation, then the born-again child of God should certainly not partake of it! But the Seventh Seal is not to be our lot, **not** because it is the Great Tribulation, but because it is the wrath of God. We, who are accepted in the Beloved, are not to partake of God's wrath.

"For God hath not appointed us to wrath, but to obtain salvation by our Lord Jesus Christ." (1 Thessalonians 5:9)

You see, the Seventh Seal cannot be the Great Tribulation because by the time the Sixth Seal (which is the Blackout) is opened, the Tribulation is over. Matthew 24:29 confirms this fact:

"Immediately after the tribulation of those days shall the sun be darkened, and the moon shall not give her light, and the stars shall fall from heaven, and the powers of the heavens shall be shaken." (Matthew 24:29)

At the risk of being repetitive, the Seventh Seal is the wrath of God which takes place in the Day of the Lord. This is evident from Revelation 6:17, when at the time of the Blackout, all who run and hide will recognize that the day of God's wrath has come. That wrath is held back in Revelation chapter seven but is released from chapter eight onwards.

Failing to recognise the Seventh Seal as the wrath of God in the Day of the Lord is one of the causes of much confusion in understanding end-time events. But you do not have to be confused anymore, because this book has made it abundantly clear by now.

THIRD MISTAKEN IDENTITY

The Jews, not the Church, will go through the Great Tribulation

---

Another common but dangerous error is made by mistaking the identity of the group of people that Jesus was referring to in a passage in Matthew chapter twenty-four.

"Then let them which be in Judaea flee into the mountains: Let him which is on the housetop not come down to take any thing out of his house: Neither let him which is in the field return back to take his clothes. And woe unto them that are with child, and to them that give suck in those days! But pray ye that your flight be not in the winter, neither on the sabbath day: For then shall be great

tribulation, such as was not since the beginning of the world to this time, no, nor ever shall be." (Matthew 24:16-21)

By now, the reader should be able to recognize that this passage is part of the description of the Fifth Seal by Jesus. There are many that believe that this passage is talking about the Jews, and not the Church, who will have to go through the Great Tribulation because Jesus mentioned *"let them which be in Judaea"* and *"pray ye that your flight be not in the winter, neither on the sabbath day"*. They contend that since Jesus used the words "sabbath day", He is referring to Jews only because only the Jews keep the Sabbath.

But take a look at the very next verse:

*"And except those days should be shortened, there should no flesh be saved: but for **the elect's sake** those days shall be shortened." (Matthew 24:22)*

This verse is a continuing statement of Jesus from the preceding verses. Jesus was saying that unless the days of the Great Tribulation be shortened, nobody is going to be saved. However, for the elect's sake, those days shall be shortened. Who is this "elect"? Does this term refer to the Jewish people? The Greek word used here is *eklektos,* which means "picked out, chosen by God to obtain salvation through Christ" (Thayer).

The word *eklektos* is used many times in the New Testament. Here are just three instances:

*"Who shall lay any thing to the charge of God's **elect**? It is God that justifieth." (Roman 8:33)*

*"Put on therefore, as the **elect** of God, holy and beloved, bowels of mercies, kindness, humbleness of mind, meekness, longsuffering; forbearing one another, and forgiving one another, if any man have a quarrel against any: even as Christ forgave you, so also do ye." (Colossians 3:12-13)*

*"**Elect** according to the foreknowledge of God the Father, through sanctification of the Spirit, unto obedience and sprinkling of the blood of Jesus Christ: Grace unto you, and peace, be multiplied." (1 Peter 1:2)*

It is very obvious from these Scriptures that both the apostles Paul and Peter were talking about the Church – the Body of Christ. It is patently clear that Jesus was addressing His beloved Church, not just the Jews alone, on the perils of the Great Tribulation. This has already been dealt with in the Fifth Seal in chapter five of this book.

Another thing to keep in mind is that the early Church, in the Book of Acts, kept the Sabbath day, which begins Friday sundown till Saturday sundown. It was only much later – many decades later – when Christianity had spread to the Roman empire, that the meeting and assembly of Christians switched to Sunday instead.

Chapter 12

THE RAPTURE - MISQUOTATIONS

Things should really begin to clear up even more by now. If you discontinue reading this book now, you would already have a good grip on the proper sequence of events leading to the Day of the Lord and thereafter. But we are not done just yet. Let us devote one more chapter to scrutinize some quotations and misquotations from Scriptures and outside of the Bible that have led to errors and confusion among Christians concerning the Rapture of the Church.

FIRST MISQUOTATION

> Enoch was raptured but Noah went through the Tribulation
> Similarly, Elijah was raptured but Elisha went through the Tribulation

Drawing from Old Testament characters, pre-tribulationists try to find support for their view with such examples as Enoch and Noah, Elijah and Elisha. According to this view, Enoch and Elijah are a type of the Church escaping the Great Tribulation by being translated to heaven without seeing death, whereas Noah and Elisha were "left behind" to go through tribulation.

Is there a parallel to be drawn from the translation of Enoch and Elijah to heaven? If any, their translation only provides a type of our hope in being raptured on the Day of the Lord when Jesus returns. To draw a parallel from Noah and Elisha is really stretching the imagination too far. First of all, both Noah and Elisha were righteous in the sight of God. If both went through the tribulation then it only goes to prove that the righteous will also go through the Great Tribulation. It's a no-brainer, really.

To consider the Flood to be the Great Tribulation is a big mistake and we have clearly seen earlier on in chapter ten of this book that the Flood is actually the wrath of God. Trying to prove that Noah went through the tribulation because he was around when God sent the flood is an exercise in futility because the flood is *not* the tribulation. Do you know what was the tribulation that Noah went through? It was the time when Noah had to endure the ridicule and persecution from the people around him for building an ark because the people at that time had never seen a flood.

Time sequence is the vital factor to consider when we want an answer to whether the righteous will escape the Great Tribulation. The establishment of a time sequence cannot be done by the quoting of a slogan. We have very systematically established the time sequence as thus:

Great Tribulation   →   Blackout   →   Rapture

The proof that the Church will go through the Great Tribulation has been established and explained, not by quoting a post-tribulationist's slogan or by hearsay, but through a clear presentation of the time sequence from the Word of God, by using Scriptures to interpret Scriptures.

SECOND MISQUOTATION

Revelation 3:10 is often quoted to support the escaping of the Great Tribulation:

*"Because thou hast kept the word of my patience, **I also will keep thee from the hour of temptation**, which shall come upon all the world, to try them that dwell upon the earth." (Revelation 3:10)*

Based on Revelation 3:10, God will allow us to escape
the Great Tribulation

Many Christians regard being kept from the hour of temptation as being kept from the Great Tribulation. Let's look at the context in which the word "temptation" is used here. While the Greek word *peirasmos* for the word "temptation" does mean trials, in this context, "temptation" is not "tribulation". Rather, temptation here refers to God's wrath and being delivered from temptation means being delivered from the wrath of God. The following Scripture will verify this:

> *"The Lord knoweth how to **deliver the godly out of temptations**, and to reserve the unjust unto the day of judgment to be punished." (2 Peter 2:9)*

The theme of Second Peter chapter two is Lot's escape from the wrath of God upon the cities of Sodom and Gomorrah. Peter ended by calling this the deliverance of the righteous from temptation. Let's read the whole passage to have a clearer understanding:

> *"And turning the cities of Sodom and Gomorrha into ashes condemned them with an overthrow, making them an ensample unto those that after should live ungodly; and delivered just Lot, vexed with the filthy conversation of the wicked: (For that righteous man dwelling among them, in seeing and hearing, vexed his righteous soul from day to day with their unlawful deeds;) **The Lord knoweth how to deliver the godly out of temptations, and to reserve the unjust unto the day of judgment to be punished.**" (2 Peter 2:6-9)*

Temptation in this context refers to the wrath of God in judgment and not the Great Tribulation. To be delivered from the hour of temptation is therefore escaping the wrath of God, not the Great Tribulation. (Thank you, apostle Peter, for coming to the rescue!)

Furthermore, Revelation 3:10 alludes to going through the Great Tribulation although the exact words are not used. Look at it again carefully:

> *"Because thou **hast kept the word of my patience**, I also will keep thee from the hour of temptation, which shall come upon all the world, to try them that dwell upon the earth." (Revelation 3:10)*

The Greek word used for the word "patience" here is *hupomone*, which means "to bear trials, to endure patiently or to suffer". Hence, the paraphrase of this verse could read: "Because you have suffered and endured patiently for My word, I will deliver you from the hour of judgment that shall come on all mankind." In other words, the Lord is saying that after the time of enduring the Great Tribulation for His word, we shall escape the wrath of God that will come upon the world.

Furthermore, the phrase *"upon all the world"* clearly tells us that Jesus was speaking of the people of the world, which means that this "hour of temptation" is only meant for everyone in the world who has rejected the saving grace of the Lord Jesus Christ. Therefore it is obvious that Revelation 3:10 cannot be quoted to support the escaping of the Great Tribulation.

THIRD MISQUOTATION

Another common reference quoted by Christians is the following Bible verse:

"Watch ye therefore, and pray always, that ye may be accounted worthy ***to escape all these things*** *that shall come to pass, and to stand before the Son of man." (Luke 21:36)*

We have been taught to believe that the expression "all these things" refer to the Great Tribulation. Hence we are taught that if we watch and pray, we shall escape the Great Tribulation and stand before the Son of man.

Jesus said in Luke 21:36 that we should pray that we can escape the Great Tribulation

---

Let us clear this misconception by answering three very basic questions. The answers to the first two questions shall establish the answer to the third question. The three questions are:

1. What are "all these things"?

2. When "all these things" have come to pass, will we still be on earth or will we be already raptured?

3. Is the Rapture the means of escaping "all these things"?

Question 1: What are "all these things"?

To answer this question, we must begin with chapter twenty-one and verse seven of the gospel of Luke:

> *"And they asked him, saying, Master, but when shall these things be?* **and what sign will there be when these things shall come to pass?"** *(Luke 21:7)*

Desiring to know when the temple in Jerusalem shall be made desolate, the disciples enquired for the sign when these things shall come to pass. Jesus then warned them of deception, wars, earthquakes, famines, and persecution. This passage is essentially the same as that of Matthew chapter twenty-four. Immediately after the Great Tribulation (Luke 21:12-24), there shall be signs in the sun and in the moon and in the stars. Obviously, this refers to the Blackout in the heavens. Jesus then said, *"And then shall they see the Son of man coming in a cloud with power and great glory."* (Luke 21:27) After this, Jesus referred to "all these things" again. Let's look at this verse carefully and we shall have the answer to our first question.

> *"And* **when these things begin to come to pass**, *then look up, and lift up your heads; for your redemption draweth nigh." (Luke 21:28)*

In Luke 21:7, they asked, "What sign will there be when these things shall come to pass?" Jesus, in verse twenty-eight, said: "And when these things begin to come to pass...." Therefore "all these things" refer to all that Jesus talked about from verse eight to verse twenty-seven of Luke chapter twenty-one. It begins with deception and ends with Jesus coming visibly in a cloud with power and great glory. Hence "all these things" in Luke 21:36 refers to all the things that will happen until Jesus comes back in power and glory.

Question 2: Will we be on earth when "all these things" take place?

The answer to this question is very simple and it is found in Luke 21:28.

> *"And when* **these things** *begin to come to pass,* **then look up, and lift up your heads; for your redemption draweth nigh."** *(Luke 21:28)*

So when "all these things" come to pass, we are still on the earth and we have not yet been raptured. However, we will be caught up at any moment when we see the Son of man coming in a cloud with power and great glory. That is why Jesus said that we are to lift up our heads and look up, for our redemption draws near.

Therefore, to claim that escaping all these things means escaping the Great Tribulation by a secret Rapture is untenable. The truth is that when "all these things" come to pass, we will still be down here on the earth.

Question 3: Is the Rapture the means of escaping "all these things"?

Answering this question is rendered academic and therefore unnecessary since the answers to the first two questions show clearly that we will not be raptured until "all these things" have come to pass. How then do we escape them according to Luke 21:36? What are the things that we are to escape? The answer is actually very obvious and it is found in verses thirty-four and thirty-five:

> *"And **take heed to yourselves**, lest at any time your hearts be overcharged with surfeiting, and drunkenness, and cares of this life, and so that day come upon you unawares. For as a snare shall it come on all them that dwell on the face of the whole earth." (Luke 21:34-35)*

To escape all these things is to escape deception, the dangers of wars and the dangers of the Great Tribulation. How shall we escape? Not by a secret Rapture but by **watching and praying**. We shall not be accounted worthy to stand before the Son of man if we are ensnared by the cares of this life and the Day of the Lord comes upon us unawares. What are the cares of this life? Putting food on the table, paying the rent or the bank instalment for your home or car, paying your utility bills and medical bills, funding your children's education, and the list goes on. There is nothing inherently wrong with these things but they can choke the life out of us if we let them. That is why they are called cares of this life. And when we get ensnared by the cares of this life, we will be very tempted and inclined to accept the mark of the beast in order for us to carry on living and surviving in this world system. Without the mark, we will not be able to do any of the aforesaid. Ponder that for a moment.

The word "escape" therefore does not mean a **non-encounter** but a **victorious encounter**. A "non-encounter" would mean avoiding the events altogether. On the other hand, a "victorious encounter" would mean facing the events but coming through unaffected and unfazed. Since "all these things" must come to pass, we cannot avoid them. Yet when "all these things" take place, we may be affected by them and be ensnared so that the Day of the Lord comes upon us as a thief in the night and we shall not be able to stand before the Son of man. We, as children of light and children of the day, ought to know better and therefore not be ensnared by "all these things". That is what 1 Thessalonians 5:1-5, which immediately follows after apostle Paul mentioned the Rapture in the preceding chapter, is actually talking about.

> *"But of the times and the seasons, brethren, ye have no need that I write unto you. For yourselves know perfectly that the day of the Lord so cometh as a thief in the night. For when they shall say, Peace and safety; then sudden destruction cometh upon them, as travail upon a woman with child; and they shall not escape. But ye, brethren, are not in darkness, that that day should overtake you as a thief. Ye are all the children of light, and the children of the day: we are not of the night, nor of darkness." (1 Thessalonians 5:1-5)*

Paul is really talking about the same thing as Jesus. He is saying that we, as believers, are not in darkness, that the Day of the Lord should overtake us as a thief. However, if we get ensnared by the cares of this world, that is "all these things", the Day of the Lord will come as a thief in the night.

Ekpheugo, the Greek word for "escape", gives us the idea of fleeing away. A look at all its occurrences in the New Testament will bring out its true meaning. There are four other passages where *ekpheugo* appears. One such occurrence is found in the following passage:

> *"But we are sure that the judgment of God is according to truth against them which commit such things. And thinkest thou this, O man, that judgest them which do such things, and doest the same, that thou shalt **escape** the judgment of God?" (Romans 2:2-3)*

In this passage, *ekpheugo* does not mean missing the judgment of God but **being found innocent** at the time of judgment. The whole concept of standing before the Son of man must be understood in the light of other portions of Scriptures. What does standing before the Son of man mean?

Malachi prophesied concerning the Day of the Lord that Jesus Christ will come suddenly like a refiner's fire.

"Behold, I will send my messenger, and he shall prepare the way before me: and the LORD, whom ye seek, shall suddenly come to his temple, even the messenger of the covenant, whom ye delight in: behold, he shall come, saith the LORD of hosts. But who may abide the day of his coming? and who shall stand when he appeareth? for he is like a refiner's fire, and like fullers' soap." (Malachi 3:1-2)

"The day of His coming" is the day He appears and "abiding His day" is to be able to stand before Him. To stand before the Son of man is therefore to abide the Day of His coming. Only righteousness (obtained through abiding faith in the finished redemptive work of the Cross) shall enable us to abide that Day when the wicked (people who have rejected the gospel of Christ) shall burn as stubble.

This is why Jesus tells us to watch and pray that we may be counted worthy to escape the snare of the things that shall surely come to pass and to stand before the Son of man. To watch and pray is to take heed to ourselves lest our hearts be overwhelmed with "all these things."

FOURTH MISQUOTATION

One of the most popular Bible verse often misquoted by many believers is 1 Thessalonians 5:2. We surmise that since the Bible says that the Day of the Lord shall come like a thief in the night, the Rapture shall be secret and invisible.

Because the Day of the Lord shall come like a thief,
the Rapture is secret and invisible

All we need to do to see whether this belief holds any water is to read that verse in its context:

"But of the times and the seasons, brethren, ye have no need that I write unto you. For yourselves know perfectly that the day of the Lord so cometh as a thief in the night. For when they shall say, Peace and safety; then sudden destruction cometh upon them, as travail upon a woman with child; and they shall not escape. **But ye, brethren, are not in darkness, that that day should overtake you as a thief.** *Ye are all the children of light, and the children of the day: we are not of the night, nor of darkness." (1 Thessalonians 5:1-5)*

When interpreting a Bible verse, we must always read that verse in its context. Failure to do so often leads to erroneous doctrines and beliefs. See what a difference it makes when you read verse two of First Thessalonians chapter five in the light of its context. It is abundantly clear that as born-again, Spirit-filled Christians, we are not in darkness as to when the Day of the Lord shall come. The apostle Paul said that the Day should not overtake us as a thief. In other words, we will not be caught unawares when the Day of the Lord comes. It only comes as a thief in the night to the people of the world because they have no idea that the first, second, third, fourth, fifth and sixth seals have been opened. For the people of the world, receiving the mark of the Antichrist would not be a big deal as they will view it as another advancement in technology for trade and commerce. The Day of the Lord will also come like a thief upon Christians who have become ensnared by "all these things" and the cares of this life which we have already dealt with in the preceding section. How will Christians be caught unawares by the Day of the Lord? Through ignorance and lack of teaching. That is why the Bible has this to say:

"My people are destroyed for lack of knowledge: because thou hast rejected knowledge, I will also reject thee…" (Hosea 4:6)

It amazes me that so many believers that I have met the world over are so caught up in the things of this life. This is what Jesus meant when He said that we are to pray and watch so that we will be counted worthy to escape "all these things". Many Christians have their mind and affection set on the affairs of this world that they have lost their passion and hunger for the things of the Spirit. During my time of interaction with such "Christians", they are very comfortable with talking about food, politics, sports, movies, history, technology and what have you. However, when it comes to talking about Kingdom matters, they will just brush you off or stare at you like you are some kind of outcast. Oh yes, they will dutifully attend church every Sunday, but there is no transformation and fruit in their lives. The Bible has this to say about them:

"This know also, that in the last days perilous times shall come. [...] Having a form of godliness, but denying the power thereof: from such turn away." (2 Timothy 3:1 and 5)

They have no desire to seek the kingdom of God and the things that are close to the Father's heart. When the Fifth Seal is opened, these "Christians" will gladly receive the mark of the Beast during the Great Tribulation so that they can go on living in this world system. For these "Christians", the Day of the Lord shall indeed come as a thief in the night upon them. By then, it will be too late. *It is in this context* that Christians (if they can really be called Christians in the first place) will not be raptured on the Day of the Lord, because they have received the mark of the Beast and worshipped the image of the Antichrist. There will *not* be a second Rapture to give them a second chance since they missed the first Rapture. This truth should be abundantly clear by now at this stage of this book.

So allow me to address this question that I posed in chapter six of this book to you again: which run shall you partake of – the first run (from the wrath of the Antichrist) or the second run (from the wrath of God)?

FIFTH MISQUOTATION

First the firstfruits, then the harvest

Among those who quote this are those who believe in two Raptures. A great man of God, for whom I have much respect, was one of those who taught this. In his book, "The Hundred And Forty-Four Thousand", he quoted from chapter fifteen of the first epistle to the Corinthians:

"But every man in his own order: Christ the firstfruits; afterward they that are Christ's at his coming." (1 Corinthians 15:23)

The order of the resurrection, according to the author, is firstly Christ, secondly the firstfruits, and thirdly they that are Christ's. Christ has already risen. The firstfruits will be raptured in a secret Rapture before the Great Tribulation while those that are Christ's will only be raptured after the Great Tribulation. Here's a chart to help illustrate his view:

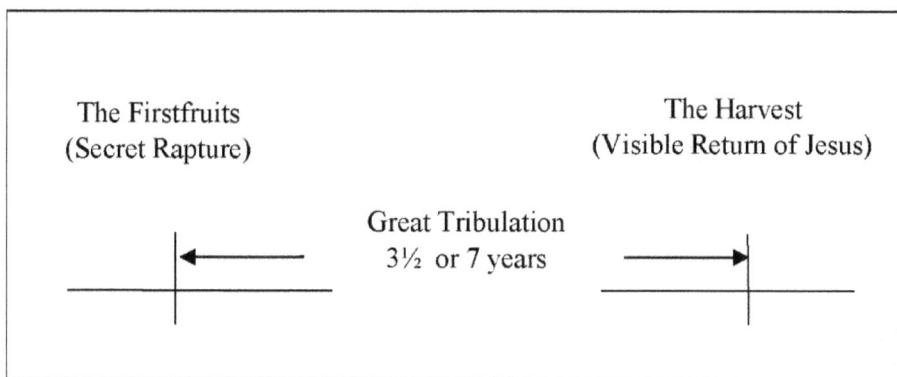

The Firstfruits   The Harvest
(Secret Rapture)   (Visible Return of Jesus)

Great Tribulation
3½ or 7 years

According to this view, the firstfruits are the saints or those that are ready for the second coming of Jesus. Those that are not ready will go through the Great Tribulation and be raptured when the Great Tribulation is over when Christ comes visibly. This view advocates a secret and invisible Rapture of the firstfruits.

But are the firstfruits actually referring to Christ or to the saints? Employing the principle of using Scripture to interpret Scripture, let us take a look at the following passage:

*"But now is **Christ** risen from the dead, and become the **firstfruits** of them that slept." (1 Corinthians 15:20)*

This verse clearly states that the term "firstfruits" is referring to Christ. I cannot over-emphasize the importance of reading a verse in the context of its chapter, in this case chapter fifteen of First Corinthians! Christ is the firstfruits of them that died. The term "firstfruits" mean *first begotten* or *firstborn*. This is established by the following passages:

> *"And he is the head of the body, the church: who is the beginning, the **firstborn** from the dead; that in all things he might have the preeminence." (Colossians 1:18)*

> *"And from Jesus Christ, who is the faithful witness, and the **first begotten** of the dead, and the prince of the kings of the earth. Unto him that loved us, and washed us from our sins in his own blood." (Revelation 1:5)*

Hence the term "firstfruits" in 1 Corinthians 15:23 qualifies Christ and does not refer to anyone else or another group. The phrase "Christ the firstfruits" therefore means that Christ is the firstfruits! The Greek text of this verse actually says: *"**the firstfruit Christ**, afterward those of Christ in the coming of Him."* (Interlinear Bible)

Therefore there are only two resurrections and not three. The first is the resurrection of Christ the firstfruits while the second is the resurrection of those that belong to Christ at His second coming on the Day of the Lord.

SIXTH MISQUOTATION

> Because God has not appointed us to wrath,
> the Church shall escape the Great Tribulation

Another oft-misquoted Scripture is taken from 1 Thessalonians 5:9:

> *"For God hath not appointed us to wrath, but to obtain salvation by our Lord Jesus Christ." (1 Thessalonians 5:9)*

Again, this assumption is based on the premise that included in the period of the Great Tribulation is the wrath of God. By now, it ought to be abundantly clear to the reader that the Great Tribulation is not the wrath of God. As God's dear children, accepted in the Beloved, God has indeed **not** appointed us unto wrath. That is why after the Blackout takes place, we are raptured. Remember the sequence: Fifth Seal (Great Tribulation), Sixth Seal (the Blackout), Seventh Seal (the wrath of God). Immediately after the Sixth

Seal is opened, the last trumpet sounds, Jesus returns and the Church is raptured.

SEVENTH MISQUOTATION

We finally come to the misquotation of Revelation chapters two and three. Many believers interpret these chapters as the seven "Church Ages". The early Church was represented by Ephesus and the Church age will end with Laodicea. Since the Church age ends with Laodicea, the Rapture of the Church must take place immediately after chapter three. Therefore many of us conclude that the Church is raptured in Revelation chapter four. The first two verses are often quoted to support this position:

"After this I looked, and, behold, a door was opened in heaven: and the first voice which I heard was as it were of a trumpet talking with me; which said, Come up hither, and I will shew thee things which must be hereafter. And immediately I was in the spirit: and, behold, a throne was set in heaven, and one sat on the throne." (Revelation 4:1-2)

They posit that from chapter five onwards, the Tribulation begins and continues until chapter eighteen. Then, in chapter nineteen, Jesus comes with the saints in power and glory. The table below sums up this view:

Revelation chapter 4	First Rapture
Revelation chapters 5-18	Great Tribulation
Revelation chapter 19	Second Rapture

There are five reasons why this view is misplaced.

First error

The first error is in interpreting the trumpet in Revelation 4:1 as the last trumpet, that is, the Rapture trumpet. We have already dealt with this in detail in chapter nine of this book. The Bible is very clear that the voice that spoke to John was **likened** unto a trumpet. It did not say it was an actual trumpet; it merely said, *"as it were of a trumpet"*. To read anything beyond that is plainly presumptuous.

Second error

The second error is in assuming that John's trip to heaven is the Rapture. You see, the Rapture does not take us to the third heaven which is the scene described in Revelation chapter four. The Rapture takes us into the physical atmosphere at cloud level.

> *"For **the Lord himself shall descend from heaven with a shout**, with the voice of the archangel, and with the trump of God: and the dead in Christ shall rise first: Then we which are alive and remain **shall be caught up together with them in the clouds, to meet the Lord in the air**: and so shall we ever be with the Lord." (1 Thessalonians 4:16-17)*

The apostle Paul makes it very clear in verse sixteen that the Lord Jesus must first descend from heaven. When Jesus returns, He descends from heaven. The Church is raptured and taken up and we will meet Him in the clouds in the air. However, Revelation chapter four is very clear that John was taken up to where the throne of God is, that is, the third heaven. It is definitely not talking about nor symbolic of the Rapture at all.

Third error

The third error is in failing to see the purpose of calling John up to heaven. He was called up so that the future might be unfolded to him. This means that there is no prophecy or unfolding of future events before Revelation chapter four. Chapters two and three of Revelation should be read as they are – they are simply seven letters of exhortation and loving rebuke and correction written to the seven churches. The process of revealing the future only began when the scroll sealed with the seven seals was opened by Jesus, the Lion of the tribe of Judah.

Fourth error

The fourth error is ignoring the fact that John was taken up in the spirit and not in the body.

> *"And immediately **I was in the spirit**: and, behold, a throne was set in heaven, and one sat on the throne." (Revelation 4:2)*

In both First Corinthians chapter fifteen and First Thessalonians chapter four, the resurrection of the body is mentioned. The dead are raised with a resurrected body and we that are alive and remain shall be changed to an incorruptible body. To aver that John's trip to heaven in the spirit is representative of the Church's rapture is simply inadmissible and insupportable.

Fifth error

The final error is the failure to recognize and understand the significance of the Sixth Seal which we have already studied in detail. The Sixth Seal is the Blackout in the heavens. Let us take one final look at this passage:

*"And I beheld when he had opened **the sixth seal**, and, lo, there was a great earthquake; and the sun became black as sackcloth of hair, and the moon became as blood; And the stars of heaven fell unto the earth, even as a fig tree casteth her untimely figs, when she is shaken of a mighty wind. And the heaven departed as a scroll when it is rolled together; and every mountain and island were moved out of their places. And the kings of the earth, and the great men, and the rich men, and the chief captains, and the mighty men, and every bondman, and every free man, hid themselves in the dens and in the rocks of the mountains; And said to the mountains and rocks, Fall on us, and hide us from the face of him that sitteth on the throne, and from the wrath of the Lamb: For the great day of his wrath is come; and who shall be able to stand?" (Revelation 6:12-17)*

It is so very clear in Matthew 24:29 that the moment this Blackout occurs, the Great Tribulation is over!

"Immediately after the tribulation of those days shall the sun be darkened, and the moon shall not give her light, and the stars shall fall from heaven, and the powers of the heavens shall be shaken." (Matthew 24:29)

I know I am beginning to sound like a broken record but the Great Tribulation is over by Revelation 6:12. To assert that Revelation chapters five to eighteen is referring to the Great Tribulation is therefore indefensible.

Chapter 13

THE ANTICHRIST

No book dealing with the book of Revelation would be complete without having at least a brief look at the person of the Antichrist. So, who is this Antichrist person? Now, when we ask this question, it does not mean we are going to embark on an exercise to speculate on the identity of the Antichrist. Rather, we want to look at his characteristics so that we will recognize him when he emerges on the world scene. Having said that, let's start with Revelation chapter seventeen.

THE BEAST THAT WAS, AND IS NOT, AND YET IS

*"And the angel said unto me, Wherefore didst thou marvel? I will tell thee the mystery of the woman, and of the beast that carrieth her, which hath the seven heads and ten horns. The beast that thou sawest **was, and is not; and shall ascend out of the bottomless pit, and go into perdition**: and they that dwell on the earth shall wonder, whose names were not written in the book of life from the foundation of the world, when they behold **the beast that was, and is not, and yet is**." (Revelation 17:7-8)*

Notice that the beginning and ending of verse eight is exactly the same but worded differently. The first part states that this beast *"was, and is not; and shall ascend out of the bottomless pit"* whereas the end of the verse states *"the beast that was, and is not, and yet is."*

Now, Revelation 20:1-2 tells us that Satan will be bound for one thousand years in the bottomless pit. This means that the bottomless pit is a maximum security prison for offending spirits. To come out of the bottomless pit will mean to come back to life again, like being released on bail. Evidently,

Revelation 17:8 is talking about a person who had been alive, and died, and will come back from the dead by ascending out of the bottomless pit.

Therefore, the first thing we need to be aware of is that the Antichrist is a person who lived, and died, and will live again. Can you see the Antichrist is a counterfeit of the Lord Jesus Christ who declared:

"I am he that liveth, and was dead; and, behold, I am alive for evermore, Amen; and have the keys of hell and of death." (Revelation 1:18)

CHARACTERISTICS OF THE ANTICHRIST

*"Now we beseech you, brethren, by the coming of our Lord Jesus Christ, and by our gathering together unto him, That ye be not soon shaken in mind, or be troubled, neither by spirit, nor by word, nor by letter as from us, as that the day of Christ is at hand. Let no man deceive you by any means: for that day shall not come, except there come a falling away first, and that **man of sin** be revealed, **the son of perdition**; Who **opposeth and exalteth himself above all that is called God, or that is worshipped**; so that **he as God sitteth in the temple of God, shewing himself that he is God**." (2 Thessalonians 2:1-5)*

From this passage, the apostle Paul informs us that the Antichrist is a man of sin. Secondly, he is called the son of perdition. This is consistent with Revelation 17:8 that describes the Antichrist as the beast who *"was, and is not; and shall ascend out of the bottomless pit, and **go into perdition**."*

Thirdly, Paul informs us that the Antichrist will have an ego that is so huge that he considers himself as God. He will oppose and exalt himself above all that is called God, or that is worshipped, so that he as God sits in the temple of God, presenting himself that he is God. This guy craves worship!

Fourthly, he will have a big mouth, a big foul mouth. Revelation 13:5-6 tells us so:

*"And there was given unto him **a mouth speaking great things and blasphemies**; and power was given unto him to continue forty and two months. And **he opened his mouth in blasphemy against God**, to blaspheme his name, and his tabernacle, and them that dwell in heaven." (Revelation 13:5-6)*

PERSECUTION OF THE SAINTS

One of the Antichrist's obsessions will be persecuting the Body of Christ, always making war against the saints.

> *"And it was given unto him to **make war with the saints**, and to overcome them: and power was given him over all kindreds, and tongues, and nations." (Revelation 13:7)*

> *"And he shall speak great words against the most High, and **shall wear out the saints of the most High**, and think to change times and laws: and they shall be given into his hand until a time and times and the dividing of time." (Daniel 7:25)*

> *"And his power shall be mighty, but not by his own power: and he shall destroy wonderfully, and shall prosper, and practise, and **shall destroy the mighty and the holy people**." (Daniel 8:24)*

Who are the saints? They are you and me; not some individuals on stained glass of some church buildings. To make war with the saints is to be against God. To be against those who belong to Christ is to be an antichrist.

Let us define the word "Christ". The Greek word for it is *christos* which means "anointed". For some reason the Greek word "christos" was never translated into the English language and was merely transliterated as "Christ". But the word actually means "anointed". Well, anointed for what? Let's go to chapter four of the gospel of Luke to find out.

> *"And there was delivered unto him the book of the prophet Esaias. And when he had opened the book, he found the place where it was written, The Spirit of the Lord is upon me, because **he hath anointed me** to preach the gospel to the poor; he hath sent me to heal the brokenhearted, to preach deliverance to the captives, and recovering of sight to the blind, to set at liberty them that are bruised, to preach the acceptable year of the Lord." (Luke 4:17-19)*

That was what Jesus was anointed for: to preach the good news to the poor, to heal the brokenhearted, to set the captives free, to restore sight to the blind, to set at liberty them that are bruised, and to preach the acceptable year of the Lord. I simply love how the prophet Isaiah sums it up:

*"And it shall come to pass in that day, that his burden shall be taken away from off thy shoulder, and his yoke from off thy neck, and the yoke shall be destroyed because of the **anointing**." (Isaiah 10:27)*

In other words, Jesus was anointed to remove burdens and destroy yokes. That is what the anointing is for. It is the burden-removing, yoke-destroying power of God! We are members of the body of Christ, which means we are members of the body of the Anointed. As members of the Body of the Anointed, you and I are anointed to carry and operate in this burden-removing, yoke-destroying power of God. That is why we are called Christians in the first place!

The devil hates the Anointing. Why? Because the Anointing destroys the works of darkness in people's lives. The Anointing removes burdens and obliterate demonic yokes in the lives of people. That is why Satan is so anti-Anointing – anti-Christ! So Satan is going to possess the Antichrist person to make war against Christians. Do you get the picture now that we have translated the word "Christ"? The body of Christ has been robbed of so much truth by never ever having the word "Christ" translated.

THE MYSTERY OF INIQUITY

We are now going to look at a very interesting description of the Antichrist which will give us a clearer revelation of who he is.

*"For the **mystery of iniquity** doth already work: only he who now letteth will let, until he be taken out of the way. And then shall that Wicked be revealed, whom the Lord shall consume with the spirit of his mouth, and shall destroy with the brightness of his coming: Even him, whose coming is after the working of Satan with all power and signs and lying wonders." (2 Thessalonians 2:7-8)*

In describing the Antichrist person, Paul called him the mystery of iniquity. He said that the mystery of iniquity was already at work. The apostle John corroborates what Paul said:

*"And every spirit that confesseth not that Jesus Christ is come in the flesh is not of God: and this is that **spirit of antichrist**, whereof ye have heard that it should come; and **even now already is it in the world**." (1 John 4:3)*

The spirit of antichrist is already working in the world through the agenda of the deep state in collusion with mainstream media. Sad to say, the spirit of antichrist is also working in some parts of the Church. Remember, the word "Christ" literally means "Anointed". When we talk about the Anointed, we have to talk about the Anointing that is upon and in the Anointed. You cannot separate the two. So every time you see opposition to the working of the Anointing of God in some churches, that is the spirit of antichrist at work. The mystery of iniquity is already at work, but it will climax in the revelation of the Antichrist person.

The word "mystery" means "hidden" or "that which is not revealed". But what is the meaning of this "mystery of iniquity"? Simply put, it is the opposite of the mystery of godliness. While the Bible does not define the mystery of iniquity, it does define the mystery of godliness. It behoves us then to look at what the Bible says about the mystery of godliness, because by doing so, we will have an understanding of the mystery of iniquity. There is only one passage in the Bible which describes the mystery of godliness.

*"And without controversy great is the **mystery of godliness**: God was manifest in the flesh, justified in the Spirit, seen of angels, preached unto the Gentiles, believed on in the world, received up into glory." (1 Timothy 3:16)*

The mystery of godliness is simply God manifesting Himself in the flesh. It is Jesus Christ Himself. Godliness was a mystery, because up until the time of the ministry of Jesus, it was not seen or revealed. Who is God? What is He like? Then finally, God came in human form and dwelt among men (John 1:14). Jesus is the manifestation of godliness – the very nature, character and ways of God dwelled in this man called Jesus of Nazareth.

In like manner therefore, the mystery of iniquity is Satan manifesting himself in the flesh. **If the mystery of godliness is Jesus Christ, then the mystery of iniquity is the Antichrist!** The mystery of iniquity therefore refers to the Wicked one revealed. That is why the word "Wicked" in 2 Thessalonians 2:8 is capitalized. This simply means that the Antichrist person is Satan manifested in the flesh. Let us realize then that the Antichrist is actually the devil possessing a man. Just as the Spirit of God was in and upon Jesus, so the spirit of Satan will be in the Antichrist.

This is why the Antichrist is also known as the son of perdition. There is only one other character in the Bible who is called as the son of perdition – Judas Iscariot. In chapter seventeen of the gospel of John, Jesus called Judas the son of perdition.

*"While I was with them in the world, I kept them in thy name: those that thou gavest me I have kept, and none of them is lost, but **the son of perdition**; that the scripture might be fulfilled." (John 17:12)*

Why did Jesus use that term on Judas? The Bible tells us that while Jesus and His disciples were having their last meal, Satan entered Judas.

"Then entered Satan into Judas surnamed Iscariot, being of the number of the twelve." (Luke 22:3)

So Judas was actually possessed by Satan, and he did what he did. Similarly, the Antichrist will be fully Satan-possessed and that is why he is also called the son of perdition.

WHO IS THIS RESTRAINER?

Now, let us return to 2 Thessalonians 2:7-8.

*"For the mystery of iniquity doth already work: **only he who now letteth will let, until he be taken out of the way**. And then shall that Wicked be revealed, whom the Lord shall consume with the spirit of his mouth, and shall destroy with the brightness of his coming: Even him, whose coming is after the working of Satan with all power and signs and lying wonders." (2 Thessalonians 2:7-8)*

We have already studied in depth the seven misquotations in the preceding chapter. This is one more passage that is used to teach that the Church will escape the Great Tribulation due to the phrase *"only he who now letteth will let, until he be taken out of the way."* It is argued that this phrase refers to the Holy Spirit who is restraining the Antichrist from appearing, and once the Holy Spirit is taken out of the way, the Antichrist will emerge. In other words, when the Antichrist comes, the Spirit of God will no longer remain in the world, and the Church will therefore no longer be around, since the Holy Spirit indwells the Church.

Now, let's ask ourselves a question. Is Satan in the world today? Yes, he definitely is. Well then, if Satan is in the world today, is the Holy Spirit also in the world now? Of course, He is! Can the Holy Spirit and Satan be in the world today at the same time? Most certainly. What then is so difficult about the Antichrist and the Holy Spirit both being in the world at the same time? What is so strange about the Church being in the world while the Antichrist is in the world? As we have seen earlier, the mystery of iniquity – the Antichrist – is already at work in the world today. The body of Christ is still here, right?

The explanation of verse seven of this passage is critical. If we say that *"he who now letteth"* is the Holy Spirit, then the Church will be raptured before the Antichrist comes. However, this interpretation contradicts an earlier verse in the same chapter of Second Thessalonians:

> *"Now we beseech you, brethren, by the coming of our Lord Jesus Christ, and by our gathering together unto him, That ye be not soon shaken in mind, or be troubled, neither by spirit, nor by word, nor by letter as from us, as that **the day of Christ** is at hand. **Let no man deceive you by any means: for that day shall not come, except there come a falling away first, and that man of sin be revealed, the son of perdition.**"* (2 Thessalonians 2:1-3)

We have already seen that the day of Christ is the Day of the Lord. What happens on the Day of the Lord? The trump shall sound, the Lord Jesus shall descend from heaven, the dead in Christ shall rise, and we who remain on the earth shall be caught up to be with the Lord in the air. The above passage of Scriptures states plainly that that Day of the Lord – the day of Christ – shall **not** come until the man of sin, the son of perdition – the Antichrist – comes first. Do you see it now? It is really not difficult to interpret the Bible; just allow Scripture to do the work of interpreting Scripture.

Who then is this "he who now letteth"? We have already seen earlier in this chapter that the Antichrist will ascend out of the bottomless pit. We have seen, from Scriptures, that he is someone who was alive but is now in the bottomless pit and will later be released to play the role of the man of sin. The bottomless pit is the lock-up where spirits are imprisoned.

The Greek word for "letteth" is *katecho* which means "to hold back, detain, retain". Therefore "he who now letteth" refers to he who is holding down or retaining the Antichrist from being released. The bottomless pit, therefore, has a keeper. Revelation chapter twenty tells us so:

> *"And I saw **an angel** come down from heaven, **having the key of the bottomless pit** and a great chain in his hand. And he laid hold on the dragon, that old serpent, which is the Devil, and Satan, and bound him a thousand years, And cast him into the bottomless pit, and shut him up, and set a seal upon him, that he should deceive the nations no more, till the thousand years should be fulfilled: and after that he must be loosed a little season." (Revelation 20:1-3)*

The Antichrist is now in the bottomless pit but he is being retained by the angel with the key. One day, the angel will step aside and release the beast and then the Wicked will be revealed. Let us therefore understand that, although it is already at work in the world now, the mystery of iniquity is being held back from manifesting himself in the fullness of his power and wickedness. Satan is not able to possess the Antichrist person yet because the latter is being restrained by the angel with the key of the bottomless pit. When that angel is taken out of the way, the mystery of iniquity will finally be revealed to the world in the flesh.

Chapter 14

OVERVIEW

Here is the time-sequence chart again to refresh your memory. It cannot be over-emphasized how important and crucial it is that we have this fully comprehended and embedded in our hearts and minds.

1st Seal DECEPTION	Rev 6:1-2 Matt 24:4-5
2nd Seal WAR	Rev 6:3-4 Matt 24:6-7
3rd Seal FAMINE	Rev 6:5-6 Matt 24:7
4th Seal DEATH	Rev 6:7-8 Matt 24:7
5th Seal GREAT TRIBULATION	Rev 6:9-11 Matt 24:9-21
6th Seal BLACKOUT	Rev 6:12-13 Matt 24:29
THE DAY OF THE LORD	1 Thess 4:15-5:2 Matt 24:30-31 Joel 2:31
7th Seal WRATH OF GOD	Rev 6:14-17 Isa 13:6-10

Where do you reckon we are in the sequence of events? It can be safely concluded that the first four seals have been opened. I firmly believe that we are witnessing the initial stages of the opening of the Fifth Seal. The sure and definite sign that the Fifth Seal is fully opened is when we see the temple of God being rebuilt in Jerusalem. Once it is rebuilt, it will only be a matter of time that the Antichrist sets up the abomination of desolation in the temple. So folks, we are only one seal away from the Sixth Seal! As I mentioned before, we are not here to determine the time-span of the Fifth Seal or any other Seal. Do note, however, that biblical prophecies do not come to pass overnight. Be that as it may, we are just one seal away from the Sixth Seal, which is the Blackout, which ushers in the Day of the Lord.

Finally, here is the lay-out of the book of Revelation.

Chapter 1   The background to the book.

Chapters 2 and 3   The seven letters to the seven churches.

Chapters 4 and 5   John taken up to Heaven to receive the revelation of future events.

Chapter 6   The revelation of the future by the unfolding of the seven seals.

The Sixth Seal is the Blackout.

The Fifth Seal is therefore the Great Tribulation period since the Blackout comes after the Great Tribulation.

*"**Immediately after the tribulation of those days** shall the sun be darkened, and the moon shall not give her light, and the stars shall fall from heaven, and the powers of the heavens shall be shaken." (Matthew 24:29)*

Chapter 7   The Rapture scene. The saints are caught up in the air before the throne (note that Jesus descends from heaven seated on His throne in Revelation 6:16).

Chapters 8, 9, 11   The wrath of God is poured out in the Seventh Seal. The scene closes with the kingdoms of this world

	becoming the kingdom of our Lord and of His Christ and the judgment of all the dead. Therefore Revelation chapter eleven ends the time sequence.
Chapter 12	The time sequence begins again with the Church going through the Great Tribulation with Satan coming against the Church through the Antichrist.
Chapter 13	Gives us the details concerning the Antichrist and his forty-two month reign.
Chapter 14	The Rapture scene followed by the pouring out of God's wrath on the armies outside Jerusalem.
Chapter 15	The preparation of the pouring out of God's wrath.
Chapter 16	The actual pouring out of God's wrath through the seven vials.
Chapters 17 & 18	The specific judgment of Mystery Babylon.
Chapter 19	The specific judgment of the armies of the world.
Chapter 20	The millennial reign of Christ ending with the Great White Throne judgment.
Chapters 21 & 22	The New Heaven and the New Earth.

There you have it. When you have the entire picture of the book of Revelation, confusion goes out the window.

Chapter 15

CLOSING EXHORTATION

It is quite obvious that not everything written in the book of Revelation has been dealt with. That is not the intention of this book. The purpose of this book is to provide the reader with the correct understanding of the proper framework and template of the book of Revelation. Once you have the macro-picture of the book of Revelation, it is easy to fill in the micro-events – the Antichrist, Mystery Babylon, the one hundred and forty-four thousand, the marriage supper of the Lamb and so on.

The following saying is somewhat cliché but when you insert the first button into the first buttonhole, the rest of the buttons will fall into place. Most Christians' understanding of the book of Revelation and end-times is like inserting the first button into the third buttonhole, the third button into the second buttonhole, and the second button into the fifth buttonhole. Imagine a shirt looking like that. That is the picture of many believers' understanding of eschatology – all twisted up and distorted – it's a mess. But if the buttons on the shirt are inserted correctly into their respective buttonholes, we get a shirt that is well laid out and we will be able to see and appreciate the shirt as it really is. It is time for Christians to come to maturity in this subject, because Jesus is coming back soon.

SO, WHAT NOW?

Some people, after reading and studying the end-times, tend to develop a "doomsday" mindset and make plans accordingly. Some believers may tend to resign themselves to the inevitability of the events spelled out in Matthew chapter twenty-four. I know of a couple who, many years ago, decided not to have children because they said that Jesus is coming back soon. In the mid-1990s, I had a friend who told me to apply for four or five credit cards and bust their credit limits as we would not have to repay the outstanding sum since Jesus is coming back soon. I would have been in serious financial trouble if I had followed this person's advice! Can you see how a skewed understanding of end-times can cause Christians to make all sorts of ridiculous decisions?

It is time to go all out for Jesus by developing a deep and intimate fellowship with our Lord and Savior in our prayer life. Intimacy with God is key in this hour. It is time to seriously heed verse twenty of the book of Jude and build up our faith by praying in the Holy Ghost. That means we need to spend more time praying in the supernatural prayer language that has been given to us by the Holy Spirit. Is it any wonder that, immediately after Jesus' discourse on the first six Seals in Matthew chapter twenty-four, He warns about having enough oil in Matthew 25:1-12? Praying in tongues will ensure that we have enough oil for ourselves like the five wise virgins. In other words, praying in tongues is *vital* in building up our inner man to have the fortitude to go through the Great Tribulation.

Another vital ingredient to have during the Great Tribulation is the joy of the Lord. I am talking about belly-laughter Holy Ghost joy! We should get rid of the idea that we have to go through the Great Tribulation somberly with a grim face. No, the joy of the Lord is our strength!

It is time to move and operate in the nine gifts of the Holy Spirit like never before, in the Church and in the marketplace. It is time to lay hands on the sick and they shall recover as Jesus promised. Yes, the first four Seals (the Beginning of Sorrows) have been opened and we are witnessing the opening of the Fifth Seal. But that does not mean that we stop preaching the good news of the Kingdom. It is inevitable that all the Seals will be opened and come to pass because it is God's Word. But the truth remains that we are to continue to proclaim what Jesus proclaimed:

"The Spirit of the Lord is upon me, because he hath anointed me to preach the gospel to the poor; he hath sent me to heal the brokenhearted, to preach deliverance

to the captives, and recovering of sight to the blind, to set at liberty them that are bruised, to preach the acceptable year of the Lord." (Luke 4:18-19)

This was, and **still is**, the primary message of Christ Jesus. As His Church, it is our honour and responsibility to continue the preaching of the burden-removing, yoke-destroying power of God to a lost and hurting world. It is really time for the Body of Christ (the Anointed and His Anointing) to grow up. When the Body of the Anointed comes to full maturity, we will see the full stature of the Anointing flowing and operating in the earth through the Church.

Let me go one further. It is time for the Church to receive the prosperity that God wants to pour into her. Why? To establish His covenant in the earth (see Deuteronomy 8:18). We live in the New Covenant and to establish the New Covenant in the earth means preaching the gospel of Jesus Christ throughout the world. Did Jesus not say in Matthew 24:14: *"And this gospel of the kingdom shall be preached in all the world for a witness unto all nations; and then shall the end come."*? Remember, He spoke these words right in the middle of the Fifth Seal, just before He spoke about the Antichrist setting up the abomination of desolation.

Now, in order to go into all the world to preach the gospel, vast amounts of finances are required. And how is the Body of Christ (that's you and me) going to have such great amount of finances? It comes by operating in the law of seedtime and harvest. We are going to have to increase the sowing of our finances so that we will reap a harvest. And remember, the harvest is always much greater than the seed sown.

Some of you are probably going, "What you are saying here is antithetical to the rest of the book!" But why should you think this way? The truth that the Church will go through the Great Tribulation does not negate other biblical truths that God wants to heal and prosper His children. They are all in God's Word. That is the problem with us believers – we somehow believe that the truth of going through trials and tribulation (including the Great Tribulation) and the truth that God wants us healthy and prosperous are mutually exclusive of each other. But that has never been, and never will be, the case in the Word of God. The truth that the Church will go through the

Great Tribulation is in the Word, supernatural healing is in the Word, praying in the supernatural prayer language of the Holy Spirit is in the Word, prosperity is in the Word.

HOW DO WE PREPARE FOR THE GREAT TRIBULATION THEN?

We have already seen that when the Antichrist implements his system, nobody will be able to buy or sell anything without his mark. As born-again children of the Most High, sealed with His Spirit, we cannot and must not receive the mark of the beast. That means we will not be able to live and operate in this world's economic system anymore. All the money that has been put into our hands will not work anymore. That is why Paul exhorts us to set our affection on things above and not on the things of the world (Colossians 3:2); and not to allow the love of money to creep in (1 Timothy 6:10). Money is just a tool for the spread of the gospel. When the time comes for us to relinquish it, no matter how much money God has put into our hands, we must be ready to let it go.

This is where we need the wisdom of God as to how we are to prepare ourselves. The Bible says that we have the mind of Christ (1 Corinthians 2:16). Christ Jesus has been made unto us the wisdom of God (1 Corinthians 1:30). The wisdom of God is already inside us and we have the mind of Christ – we will therefore know what to do.

This book is not going to tell you to do this and that, or invest in this and that. But I will say this: get out of debt. And remain out of debt. God's people should be self-sufficient. God's Word tells us so:

"And God is able to make all grace (every favor and earthly blessing) come to you in abundance, so that you may always and under all circumstances and whatever the need be self-sufficient [possessing enough to require no aid or support and furnished in abundance for every good work and charitable donation]." (2 Corinthians 9:8, AMPC)

God wants us to have complete sufficiency, requiring no aid, especially during the Great Tribulation. That means complete sufficiency in terms of food, land and resources. Most importantly, bear in mind that while the world grows darker and darker culminating in the Sixth Seal, the path of the just shines brighter and brighter unto the perfect Day (Proverbs 4:18).

WHAT HAPPENS AFTER THE RAPTURE?

We often stop at Rapture and do not contemplate what happens next. After the Church is caught up to meet the Lord Jesus Christ in the air, that is not the end of it. We are not going to be floating on soft white clouds singing a cute little song with little harps in our hands. Revelation chapters nineteen and twenty tell us otherwise:

> *"And the armies which were in heaven followed him upon white horses, clothed in fine linen, white and clean. And out of his mouth goeth a sharp sword, that with it he should smite the nations: and he shall rule them with a rod of iron: and he treadeth the winepress of the fierceness and wrath of Almighty God." (Revelation 19:14-15)*

> *"Blessed and holy is he that hath part in the first resurrection: on such the second death hath no power, but they shall be priests of God and of Christ, and shall reign with him a thousand years." (Revelation 20:6)*

We will return together with the King of kings and Lord of lords to the earth to reign and rule with Him. What does that mean? It means the Commander-in-Chief will delegate His authority and power to you and me to govern and administer wherever you and I live throughout the earth. Jesus Himself will rule and reign from Jerusalem but you and I will be appointed to govern and administer over counties, towns, cities, provinces, states and entire countries. Exciting, isn't it?

FINAL WORD

When it comes to studying the end-times, never use current world events to interpret Scriptures. We are to use Scriptures to interpret world events. This principle will keep us from coming up with all sorts of conclusions. Some rivers have turned red (due to some kind of algae) and over-enthusiastic believers start claiming that the vials of God's wrath have been poured out. If the vials have been poured out, the Church would not be here on earth anymore! Can you now appreciate how absolutely crucial a proper and systematic understanding of the book of Revelation is? When someone tells you that one of the bowls have been poured out, you can now rest in the knowledge that that is not true because you now have the correct understanding of the sequence of events.

One should not become fearful after having read the book of Revelation. Rather, one should become confident, assured, and grounded after reading it. It is my prayer that this book has helped you, the reader, achieve that.

On that note, let's close with these Scriptures:

"Being confident of this very thing, that he which hath begun a good work in you will perform it until the day of Jesus Christ." (Philippians 1:6)

"And the very God of peace sanctify you wholly; and I pray God your whole spirit and soul and body be preserved blameless unto the coming of our Lord Jesus Christ." (1 Thessalonians 5:23)

Even so, come, Adonai Yeshua.

For more information contact:

Joseph Loh
jltlministries@gmail.com

To purchase additional copies of these book visit our online bookstore at:
www.advbookstore.com

*A*dvantage
BOOKS

Saint Johns, Florida, USA
we bring dreams to life™
www.advbookstore.com

For more information contact:

Joseph Loh
jltlministries@gmail.com

To purchase additional copies of these book visit our online bookstore at:
www.advbookstore.com

*A*dvantage
BOOKS

Saint Johns, Florida, USA
we bring dreams to life™
www.advbookstore.com